**WITHDRAWN
UTSA LIBRARIES**

NOT FOR THE RECORD
Selected speeches and writings

LORD GOODMAN

NOT FOR THE RECORD

Selected speeches and writings

Preface by Lord Annan

ANDRE DEUTSCH

First published 1972
by André Deutsch Limited
105 Great Russell Street London WC1

Copyright © 1972 by Lord Goodman
All rights reserved

Printed in Great Britain
by Ebenezer Baylis and Son Ltd
The Trinity Press, Worcester, and London

ISBN 0 233 96346 4

TO MY BROTHER

Contents

Preface by Lord Annan ... 9

PART ONE: Personal Freedom and Individual Liberty

1. Erosions of Personal Freedom in a Modern Society ... 17
2. Takeovers and the Employee ... 32
3. A Plea for the Small Business ... 37
4. Abolition of the Death Penalty ... 41
5. Student Participation in Higher Education ... 47
6. Race Relations in Britain ... 51
7. Divorce Reform ... 53
8. Rhodesia – The Settlement Proposals ... 57

PART TWO: The Institutions

1. Reform of the House of Lords ... 69
2. The Press ... 73
3. Law Reform ... 77
4. Administration of Justice ... 86
5. Solicitors' Spirit of Indignation ... 92
6. The City of London Court ... 96
7. The Biafran War (I) ... 103
8. The Biafran War (II) ... 111

PART THREE: The Arts

1. In Place of Censors ... 117
2. Arts Council Reports, 1967–70: The Chairman's Introduction ... 120
3. The Arts in Britain ... 131

CONTENTS

4 Jennie Lee: Minister 139
5 Public Lending Right and Regional Subsidy 142
6 The Book and the Patron 147
7 A Fair Deal for Authors 157
8 The Arts Council and the New Activists 160
9 Obscenity and the Arts 163
10 Pornography in Britain 168

Postscript 173

Preface

Arnold Goodman suffers from an identity crisis—though the sufferer is not him but the public. The most recognizable figure in national affairs, he flits in and out of the country unidentified, to the mortification of reporters. An attempt was made in 1964 when he helped to settle the commercial television strike to keep his name secret by Mr Wilson who 'described me as Mr X in great kindness because he thought it would save me from being identified. That was one of his few naiveties'. The next year Goodman was made a life peer and Chairman of the Arts Council. Until that year he had never made a speech in public since he was an undergraduate. He has certainly made up for lost time, and the variety of topics on which he speaks are more than matched by his activities as conciliator and advocate of good causes behind the scenes. Ever since, the publicists have been trying to paste a label on him.

None of the labels stuck. That is not because Arnold Goodman is protean: his character is all of a piece. But it is not easy to define and, though some will find the simile far-fetched, he slips like an eel through your fingers. To call him a fixer or an *eminence grise* explains nothing. He knows many rich men—and that money does not banish boredom. He mixes with the powerful—but is more aware of the limitations of their power than of their importance. He does not himself love power or enjoy manipulating the levers of government in Whitehall or in the Establishment. He has no overt ambition, no programme, no intention of mobilizing political support. He enjoys dining out but is without social pretensions.

He is a liberal; but he disappoints numbers of other liberals, many progressives and, still more, all radicals. He will not sign the liberal ticket which says that those who support one good cause should support the lot. Package deals are not for him: he insists on using his intelligence on each problem as it comes up.

For, unlike so many liberals, Arnold Goodman knows that if you care passionately about liberty in one aspect, you are going to have to admit that liberty in another sphere is less important. And there is no doubt which sphere he thinks most important. It is the liberty and dignity of the individual.

Just as he demands privacy for himself, he demands that men and women should not be smeared, traduced and blackened by the Press and the media. He may be Chairman of the Newspaper Proprietors Association but he has not lost his sense of outrage at seeing, as over the years he saw in his law office, the scandalous allegations made about those who come to him in distress. Like Cassio, he thinks a man's reputation is the immortal part of himself. Admittedly at the time of the Profumo affair Lord Denning had to examine whether a Minister of the Crown had endangered the safety of the state: but in Goodman's opinion the rest of the report was a disgraceful and unnecessary excursion, 'the investigation of rumours is a grievous invasion of personal liberty'. In the disturbance at certain universities he was far from thinking that the authorities behaved wisely: but the vilification by the militant students of their teachers he regarded as odious. To him the first task of education is to produce civilized human beings.

As legal adviser to several of the leading members of the Labour Government, he is labelled as a man of the Left. Here again the label fell off. He distrusts egalitarianism. The Left believe that legislation is often necessary to remedy injustice and disparity between social classes. Arnold Goodman is sceptical of regulations. Like many lawyers, he doubts the power of laws to improve man's lot. Many regulations can be shown certainly to restrict the liberty of some, and cannot be shown as conclusively to increase the liberty of others. 'Injury to an individual,' he wrote, 'is an injustice to the community in whose name it is so lightly committed.'

Enlightened opinion declared that English juries need no longer be unanimous to reach a verdict: Goodman regretted the change. Enlightened opinion thought that the City of London Court on which only aldermen sat should be abolished: Goodman joined the powerful lobby to resist the reform, on the grounds that the Court in its present form worked well enough—and won. No one these days says much for the small business man: in this age of nationalized industries, great corporations and mergers, Goodman extolled his virtues and sung a threnody over his passing. Many sensible dons believe that students should participate in running universities: Goodman denounced it as humbug. Politicians of all parties reject out of hand the notion of a national newspaper receiving a state subsidy: Goodman envisages it as natural as a subsidy to the BBC. Many people have been surprised that a man who voted against the 1971 Immigration Bill should go a few weeks later as the Government's principal negotiator in Rhodesia. But Goodman thought that as there was not the faintest chance of a revolution which would put the African majority in power, it was a lesser evil to alleviate their lot and get as good a settlement as could be got in a bad situation than to accept an economic stagnation which could lead only to a greater degradation of the African population.

But there is no doubt where his heart lies. The reform of the laws on capital punishment, homosexuality, abortion or divorce — all those situations in which human beings in anguish can be helped by a change in the law — have his support. He never doubted that the censorship of the Lord Chamberlain should go, though he hesitated for a moment, wondering whether a voluntary scheme operated by theatrical managements might not be useful: when he failed to get support for the notion he abandoned it — 'it is better to think yourself mad than the rest of the world mistaken'. In fact he has no patience with the obscenity hounds: the dangers of pornography, he thinks, are inflated. He is that rarest of reformers — the man who thinks that his own profession needs to be reformed. To him the division between barristers and solicitors is costly to the public, bad for justice — and insulting to solicitors. When his friend, Lord Gardiner, in a flow of genial banter, implied in the House of Lords that if solicitors were made circuit judges, the worst excesses of American courts might be reproduced in Britain, Lord Goodman was on his feet in a flash and rebuked him with some asperity. And why, he has asked on another occasion, for good measure, does not the Court of Chancery which deals with wardship and infancy cases, ever appoint a woman judge? The *bien-pensants* mutter over him and fume at his success.

He is not an intellectual. The speeches and articles in this book

are not profound statements of truth. He does not compete with
Sir Isaiah Berlin or Professor Herbert Hart. There is nothing
original here about justice or liberty or art. But he has the most
precious of gifts which intellectuals often lack: he has wisdom.
What you see in the book is these great concepts in full spate,
rivers flowing over barrages and waterfalls with Goodman
occasionally breaking up a log jam. Under him the Arts Council
has had no pretensions to control, direct or give birth to art. It is
not a mother, but a mid-wife, and a mid-wife who should know
her place. Artists are exceedingly important people in any society
which pretends to be civilised. 'No undue control should ever
be exercised over the people to whom the benefits are given.' One
of Goodman's concerns has been to provide funds for the arts
outside London, but he denies that there is an operation room in
the Arts Council with a map covered in flags, or that the Secretary
General is heard to murmur, 'Culture is lagging in Westmorland.
There is a recession of the higher sort in Cumberland.'

His humour envelops him. As he enters a party, like a great
tanker edging towards her moorings, bonhomie, good-will,
warmth, friendliness, and even a touch of fantasy, radiate through
the room. People perk up and look happier. He menaces no one:
that is why politicians like him. The large face, creased with
benignity, the lift of the eyebrows and the expression of amused
expectation, remind you of portraits of David Garrick—magnified. 'Every so often,' he says, 'I lose a little weight, and to my
utter horror and indignation, I find in the quiet of the night
somebody has put it back again.'

Charm is a quality which men in public life are often said to
have. Usually they imitate a charm they never had, just as tired
people imitate the charm they once had but have lost. Charm is
magical and subtly connected with vitality. Arnold Goodman has
charm, and the paradox is that for the worldly man that he is,
his charm is tinged with innocence and wonder. Like other Jews
he loves to give, but he has enough self-awareness to know that
those who are known to be charming and prodigal with their gifts
will be ruthlessly exploited unless they are on their guard.
Publicity is his affliction: for years he refused to appear on television. 'I don't regard myself as a public entertainer.' Yet in fact
he is one of the greatest speakers in England. He has only to rise

in the Lords and they crowd in to hear him. He speaks with hardly a note, at great speed, with unshakeable conviction, bravura and assurance. He reasons. He enchants. His courtesy is proverbial. This, too, is how he negotiates. Successful negotiators are often supposed to be wily, supple individuals skilled at driving a coach and four round rather than through the maze of the law. Goodman's success is the very reverse: it 'is achieved by not using any tricks'. What matters is frankness, saying in great detail what his side can afford to give and where their hands are genuinely tied. What matters is that each side should have confidence in the other.

He inspires confidence. This foreword will disappoint those who hoped for some revelation about his inner life. I do not know him intimately nor have I known him for long, but my confidence in him is boundless. All I know is that if I were in trouble, and worse, if I were in disgrace, I should go to him. For this there is a simple reason. He can burn with indignation at examples of human folly, stupidity, ingratitude and cruelty. But in his concern for human beings he does not forget that the benighted, the oppressors, even criminals, have still a vestige of human dignity and must not be treated as dirt. 'Nothing that is totally sincere can be totally ridiculous,' he once said, and it is a dictum that has more overtones and implications than are at first sight apparent. Time and again when I watch him holding forth, bringing all his legal expertness to bear upon a small point which is small yet central to some issue of personal dignity, I recall a line of poetry which he may have heard as an undergraduate at Cambridge when the play was acted in Greek—the words Antigone speaks to Kreon: 'My nature is to join in love, not to hate.'

NOEL ANNAN

PART ONE

Personal Freedom and Individual Liberty

1. Erosions of Personal Freedom in a Modern Society

It is egotistical to believe that one has better powers to see what is going on around one than are shared by one's fellow men. This I do not believe, but I do believe that certain people through chance may find themselves situated at particular vantage points well designed to give a full panoramic view of the social picture which may well be denied to others working industriously in the valleys without the energy or the inclination to ascend occasionally to the hill-tops for a view across the horizon.

It is because the many activities in which I am engaged include those of an observer that I have had cause to see developments, trends and tendencies which, although noticed and remarked upon by a significant number of people, are still not sufficiently the subject of general comment and perhaps of general warning.

My address to you today claims no special profundity and could claim none. It concerns subjects on which I am not an expert. It deals with political, social and philosophical conceptions in which my own qualifications are exiguous, but the role that I have assumed for myself I hope enables me to embark lightly on these topics in the situation of someone who is genuinely in quest of information, anxious to pose the questions but not in the least pretending to know the answers. But I do believe them to be important questions.

First, let me make clear that the title of this lecture, selected some while back before it was composed as a broad general indication of its nature, is too wide and too imprecise; it is misleading in that it may convey much more than my present feelings. I do not believe that we are living in a slave state; I do not believe that we can no longer breathe in relative liberty – allowing the constrictions of fog and smoke. I believe that in comparison, and all too often in contrast, with too many other countries, we enjoy freedom and can still be boastful of it. The basic essential of freedom of government – the right to eject one set of rulers and install another – has not been tampered with. It remains the touchstone of a free society. But it requires a devout constitutionalist to appreciate the immeasurable value of the elective system and to disregard or diminish the 'goings on' between the elections that I believe to be so discouraging to great numbers of people. Nor does the comfort of the electoral emancipation from disliked measures and rules operate effectively unless there is faith that the new rulers will adopt different methods – will not offend in the way of their predecessors. But the encroachments on liberty which I report have no political origins. Both parties are equally at fault – they are becoming a built-in element of government and, with diffidence, I suggest are becoming a built-in vice of government.

For I believe that slowly and imperceptibly governments – as a part of the governmental process – are taking away essential liberties. They are doing it unashamedly and without apology, either by statutory or legal changes, or more insidiously through economic development carrying such deprivations in their wake.

I believe that the consciousness that we are living in a society where liberty of individual action is diminishing constantly is making a marked effect on younger people. That the unrest and malaise that do exist, the unsatisfactory relationship between the young and the mature, in part at least, may be due to an increasing sense of social claustrophobia that the young may sense and feel without positive identification. And if they are subject to such sensations, there is, I believe, ample and increasing justification for it.

The topic is a vast one and only the briefest summary can be provided within the period of endurance of the best trained of lecture audiences. It is in addition immensely controversial. A reasoned and convincing defence would be supplied for each count of any indictment. It would, I think, be based largely on the popular proposition that we must sink our selfish self-interest in the public good, that *salus populi suprema lex*, and that although individuals may suffer they should do so uncomplainingly for the benefit of the community. Now of all governmental propositions requiring the closest scrutiny and the strongest scepticism, this one comes foremost. For it is the proposition which can justify

EROSIONS OF PERSONAL FREEDOM

any hardship or injustice to a private person – and the one most prone to ignore the arithmetical truism that the community is the sum of its individuals. That injury to an individual – inequitable or unrequited – is, in the absence of strong contrary proof, an injustice to the community in whose name it is so lightly committed. But it is invoked with monotonous ruthlessness by governmental systems which – in their frenzied haste to maintain a steady, even flow of new legislation – have forgotten, if they ever knew, the purpose of government, and which confuse the pure self-indulgence of unrestricted legislative activity with a pathetic belief that all legislation flowing from a present government (as distinct from its predecessor) is a social virtue – for which only ingrates such as your present lecturer will not give dutiful thanks. But I do not give thanks and I would urge that we should none of us give thanks for governmental energy and zeal as disembodied qualities. For I do believe that nothing does more to induce social insecurity, frustration, and in the end discontent than an endless flow of legislative change, and this aspect of society I would place first in my catalogue of the matters upon which we need to shine the searchlight of an enlightened reformist spirit.

Each year, with increasing volume – and terrifying diligence – whatever government may happen to be in power will enact Statutes by the dozen creating new restrictions, and new offences; changing the law with little or no regard for established rights; putting into effect a programme whose seeming beneficence, viewed from the comfortable pages of an election address, may be more than neutralized by the injury of change to great numbers of people. Every year we have a Budget – translated into a Finance Act – designed by the wizard in charge to make us happier and in the very long run richer. But every year, with a callousness which is the more frightening because it is unintended and unconscious and to him totally unimportant, sections of the community may be ruined overnight. Illustrations are too readily available and too painful. The fluctuation in a travel allowance – which occurs with gay abandon every time it is desired to demonstrate that the pampering influence of holiday travel cannot be countenanced under our successive puritan regimes – will damage or destroy the trade of agents, hoteliers, and other innocent people at home and in many parts of the world. A change in tobacco duty may enrich or ruin the tobacconist; a change in purchase tax teaches the furrier or jeweller to know better than to indulge the appetite of luxury when austerity is the payment. But we may ask whether such fiscal caprice is either just or even sane; can a society regard itself as well ordered which damages or destroys innocent members overnight – without a word of warning or a word of regret or a whisper of compensation? Can the injured members regard themselves as living in circumstances of guaranteed freedom when so arbitrary an act can be so inflicted? I pose the question and ask no answer.

But in extenuation of Budget and Revenue changes government can plead that habitual misfortune which – apparently however skilled the economist concerned – inevitably leaves a situation of crisis for resolution by measures of near-hysteria at least twice a year, and now seemingly oftener. We may therefore decide to forgive the peremptory nature of financial legislation – and we are in these matters forgiving beyond credence. But should we forgive the continued flow of Acts of Parliament which year after year – creating virtually no liberties – erode gently and persistently the diminishing hurdle of liberties that we still possess? It is easy to appear flippant about them. It may be regarded as positively unserious to list a few of the novelties of 1967. It is a risk I will assume, since 1967 was not specially a bumper year – but it provided a fair average crop from which to make a judicious selection.

An intense code of new law was introduced by the creation of a Land Commission, an Act of undoubted social potential, open to detailed criticism, but, more important, open to the contention that it was enough for the year on its own. It radically altered the rights of every landowner. It needed to be absorbed slowly and methodically by a population which could barely be apprised of it – and to this day is barely apprised of it – before the continuing flood of additional laws drowned even the massive bulk of this one. For the year, of course, introduced the breathalyzer. Very good, many will say, and I should echo them. But before you could savour the benefit of this splendid and adventurous piece of law along came wage restraint; and, good or bad, there flowed after it livestock marketing control for farmers; and the necessity for a licence (for the first time) for a private place of entertainment run for gain; to sell a dead wild goose; to take a lapwing's egg (without need of a licence from the lapwing); to give driving lessons; to hold a shot-gun; to pick flowers in Antarctica. If you run a restaurant, you may be required to close at 11 p.m.; if you sell television sets you must report your customers (a provision in line with the other obligation of delation, for a doctor to report his drug addict patients – regardless of the relationship of doctor and patient whose confidence is a long hallowed tradition of civilized living). But, to continue the year, Statute required you to keep away from pirate radio – in terms appropriate for an act of high treason – since to bring any comfort by way of victuals or other aid was an offence in itself, although you might mercifully rescue them if they were sinking. You must not, since 1967, kill your turkey except in an approved manner – again not necessarily approved by the turkey. You must not, in this year of light, dump your car in the open. You may not (although until stopped you may) supply, acquire or consume liquid fuel, or sell plant food without the prescribed label. You may be arrested for crime on a British controlled aircraft; if a preserved tree on your land dies, you must plant another.

It is demonstrably a year of serious restriction of liberties for pirate musicians and felonious air-passengers; of grave diminution for land-owners; of relevant increases in the liberties of lapwings, turkeys, and dead geese (wild); and of gentle encroachment and erosion for the average citizen. But in justice not all was debit in the account book of freedom. It was the year which, wisely and mercifully, made consenting adults (of over 21) free to engage in their own sexual practices; abortion was made a social possibility in circumstances of confused uncertainty and insecurity, and you can no longer be prosecuted for being an eavesdropper or a common scold – a reform which many may regard as highly retrograde.

You may ask – and seemingly with reason – whether these matters (and the many others I have mentioned) seriously affect the ordinary human being. The answer, I believe, is that they do. That most people, like yourselves, will know nothing of these changes until one of them wants to open a private place of entertainment, buys a television set and finds that his supplier is also an honorary state informer, or does one of the relatively obscure acts that until 1967 had somehow remained unprescribed without apparent damage to the structure of society.

And, each year (be the government Socialist or Tory, coalition or of one unsullied texture) the endless stream proceeds. Nor does the citizen complain or even I complain on his behalf where, however onerous, the statutory requirement is tied in with some governmental policy. The law now requires tax returns so comprehensive that only the immortal soul may be left undisclosed – and certain it is that any trafficking with it by a modern Dr Faustus would attract a capital gains tax for the increased earning capacity of his revitalized person. But these – albeit with muttering – we accept as necessary for the machine of government. But all the others – are they necessary? Should we accept them as lightheartedly as we do? Are we satisfied that any present-day government realizes the weighty responsibility that attaches to a legislative change which leaves us – even by a featherweight – less free than when it was introduced?

Nor are the changes always in areas of obscurity or superficial unimportance. Last year saw the disappearance of the unanimous jury and the acceptance of a lower standard of justice – a majority verdict. I voted in favour of the measure with misgivings. It was presented as a necessity for the proper administration of justice against the resourceful and audacious manœuvres of professional criminals – now embarked on the bribing of juries. The evidence seemed to establish the case – but the measure was not one for rejoicing but for a reception with heavy heart that a liberty enshrined in the fabric of British justice was now somewhat frayed – had had to be tampered with. I heard no one in authority present the matter in this light and I regretted this as much as the departed unanimity.

Nor in the struggle against increasing lawlessness was the change in our jury system the only unhappy, if unavoidable, development. The law of criminal libel – over the years regarded as an erratic and dangerous instrument and brought into almost total disrepute by a famous First War trial of one Pemberton Billing – was reintroduced in circumstances that can give little satisfaction and much disquiet to liberty lovers. A prosecution was instituted on behalf of members of the police force against accused persons who had made allegations of ill-treatment against the officers concerned in connection with their arrest or detention. The men were convicted and sentenced to terms of imprisonment – convictions which were disrelated from the original offences with which they were charged. I do not question the verdict in the case. I question the wisdom of allowing the police force a preferential form of protection against personal defamation, and allowing the existence of a weapon available in retaliation against charges which in any civilized society no man should be deterred from making by the introduction of new penalties and new sanctions.

I made a solitary protest against this at the time when it happened. I am unrepentant about referring to it again. The practice has not been repeated and it is my earnest hope that it will not be repeated. The civil law of libel is clumsy and laborious and should be invoked only in circumstances where a man's reputation is in serious jeopardy if he fails to protect it – the rarest of occurrences – but it is the normal instrument used by the entire population to defend its character and it is as much available to officers of the police as to others; more so, since very properly in such circumstances the burden of expense incurred by a libel action – for which assistance by legal aid is not available – would be borne by the authorities on behalf of their police members.

Nor should I fail to mention what brings me directly to my second category of invasions of freedom, those which relate to personal character and personal privacy. This is no new development. On the whole we are better now than we were in the eighteenth century in the way of protecting the reputations of innocent people. The law of libel, although as I have said cumbersome and inartistic, is an effective deterrent when operating in proper circumstances. But it is important, in my view, to recognize its value in a free society to preserve freedom. The freedom from being traduced is as much a freedom as the freedom to criticize. No one would wish for one second to prevent the most vehement criticism, and anyone concerned, even mildly, in public life is aware that this liberty is generously exploited, but on the whole the British Press has maintained an honourable tradition in distinguishing between a man's private life and his public activities. There are signs that in certain quarters the distinction might become blurred and the healthy, moral effect of the law of libel ought not to be diminished in preserving the clear edge.

There is a vigorous campaign conducted on behalf of newspapers – and none the worse for that since there is no concealment of its origins – to mitigate the law of libel by introducing new defences. I will not enter in detail into a debate which has been conducted with energy and tolerable success elsewhere in seeking to resist these changes. The major change that has been proposed is that there should be added to the defences of truth and fair comment on a matter of public concern a further defence that, although the statement made in the event turned out to be untrue, it was believed to be true on reasonable grounds at the time of publication. The arguments for this defence are attractive and, of course, especially attractive to the newspaper. The contention is that, where some public scandal is concerned, a newspaper or journal will be deterred from disclosing information it possesses at a stage earlier than might otherwise be the case because at present it is at risk until it has doubly confirmed its accuracy, and thereby the public may be injured because some malpractice is not stopped the sooner, some spy not apprehended in better time. This is an attractive argument but in my view specious. It totally disregards the position of the innocent victim against whom the charge is made precipitately and without final proof and who emerges thereafter as guiltless of it. There may be circumstances in which the public interest demands that a man's reputation be risked *pro bono publico*, but in such cases is it unreasonable to ask that, if a newspaper is sufficiently convinced of its facts to be prepared to seek to destroy a man's reputation, it should be prepared to accept the financial responsibility if it perpetrated so gross an error? 'Publish and be damned' is a brave and worthy slogan: 'publish and let your victim be damned' is of more dubious moral quality, for it must be remembered that not least of the dangers to our liberties is the diminution in the number of newspapers, that a high measure of protection exists in a society which has multiple outlets for news and comment readily available to contradict each other's errors and opinions. But for reasons that are shrouded in mystery, even to those who closely investigate the situation, a national newspaper today can only survive with a mammoth circulation, and papers selling upwards of two million copies a day to their readers are reported to be struggling against financial odds. We have lost several newspapers. We remain threatened with the loss of several others. Certain it is that if more and more become vested in fewer hands, as has become the unavoidable situation, the rights of the individual are open to the risk of jeopardy even if the quality and integrity of the papers concerned afford a present protection. We are told that it would be a grave encroachment on our freedom to seek to support any newspapers from national funds. This may be the case. Certainly it would require the most careful and cogent investigation of any such step, but we should, I think, at least keep open minds as to whether such a step – suitably regulated and placed for administration in the hands of disinterested people – is not to be preferred to further mortalities in the free Press. Again I pose the question. The answer is a difficult one.

The one certainty is that fewer newspapers mean fewer liberties. With a concentration of ownership, there are fewer editorial desks where a disgruntled or dissatisfied editor – determined to take his coat off the peg and seek employment elsewhere – can find such employment. To constrict that choice too closely is to damage liberty in its most vulnerable kind. It is to damage all our conceptions of freedom of speech and freedom of expression.

Nor does it suffice to point out that any particular owner does not interfere with editorial policy and that the multiple ownership of newspapers in one proprietor can be regarded as equivalent to dispersed ownership because of the individual discretions bestowed on each editor. This is self-deception. The proprietor may regard the editor as free, but no editor capable of ordinary speech can regard himself as free if he does not set eyes on his proprietor from one year's end to another. The comfortable shadow continues to inhibit the real freedom that a free Press demands, and how inhibiting and how frustrating and galling to the young that no new newspaper and no new periodical can be established from independent resources. The cost is so formidable, the risks so great, that unless one of the great publishing organizations is prepared to subsidize and support the venture, its prospects of being launched are slender. Very occasionally a brave band of pioneers will produce a publication in blurred print which somehow stays alive in defiance of all economic laws. To them, almost regardless of the contents of the publication and almost regardless of any penchant for defamation that its circulation may demand, I extend my hearty congratulations. The survival of any unsubsidized paper which is not a subsidiary of another paper, itself a subsidiary of yet another, is a contribution to free life.

But in the field of personal reputations the most startling and least remarked upon phenomenon of recent years was the Denning Report, following upon the security alarms and excursions arising from the rather ubiquitous activities of one young lady.

All this is ancient history, and even to revive the recollection of the facts would be distasteful to me and to everyone present, but the Denning Report is an incident in itself which historically will be the subject of scrutiny and comment for generations to come. It will, I hope, be remarked upon by historians that some people in this generation regarded aspects of it with astonishment, considered it to be a precedent that ought not to have been established, and hoped with urgency that we should never see its like again. None of this in the least reflects on the extraordinary brilliance and social judgement of the author of the report, Lord Denning. On the contrary, the document might well have been historically infamous but for the matchless skill, discretion, and good taste with which he conducted a task which no one should have been asked to conduct. He saw to it that the document did not erode the liberties of the individuals concerned more than was indispensable for the proper discharge of his duties, but in other hands I shudder to think how the matter might have been conducted, or what damage now and in the future it could have done to our political institutions.

I do not, of course, allude to the bulk of the report, which was concerned with investigating very properly whether or not there had been a security situation created out of facts established sufficiently to give rise at least to a prima facie case for anxiety, but I do refer to the second part of the report, which although of commendable brilliance has no parallel in English published public documents, for it was an investigation of rumours which affected the honour and integrity of public life. Many of us may have forgotten the low point of public morale which had been reached at the time of these matters, the multiplication of rumour upon rumour, the whispers that were going around about almost everyone under the sun, the whispers that were going around about this or that alleged scandal. It is precisely in such an atmosphere of moral vulnerability that robust public institutions stand their ground. At some stage someone should have said with firmness and even violence, 'It will be a sorry day when public men are exposed to the investigation of any rumour that any scurrilous tongue cares to invent. No House of Parliament is going to instruct any tribunal to engage in such an investigation. The public investigations will be restricted to situations where a prima facie case exists to establish that there are matters that may cause public mischief and which need to be followed up.' This and this alone should be the scope of public inquiry, and such inquiries should be and must be conducted in the cleansing air of publicity. A man may keep his private life to himself, but the ventilation of a public scandal must be by public scrutiny.

I had the honour to be a member of a Royal Commission, brilliantly chaired by Lord Justice Salmon, to report upon tribunals of inquiry in general. We produced a report in record – almost Olympic – time, but we might have spared ourselves our exertions, since of all the matters that the Government appears concerned to expedite, this one seems to lack any attraction. We produced what I believe was a simple straightforward document. We recommended that no Denning-type inquiry should ever be conducted again; that no inquiry should take place except into matters which on the face of them justified inquiry, for the investigation of rumours is a grievous invasion of personal liberty. No one has known this better than the late Titus Oates and the late Senator McCarthy, and at that point in our history we came very near to reproducing almost ideal conditions for these expert practitioners in calumny. But we have created a precedent that I believe we need publicly to expunge. There ought not even historically to be suspended over the heads of British public men the threat that at some time another government may decide to involve them in investigations about reports or rumours that are quietly put about. I hope some means is found of effacing this precedent by such public pronouncement. I think it is a matter that touches liberty at its very heart. It is to nobody's credit that the inquiry was not vigorously challenged, but we can, I think, regard it as a species of midsummer madness that we can all fervently hope that we shall not encounter again, for the corollaries of such products of hysteria and frenzy are bound to be no less discreditable. After the inquiry there ensued a trial which did no credit to British justice. The episode demonstrated once again the unshakeable axiom that the practices and procedures of generations should not be changed through a momentary panic.

I have spoken up to now of matters of a public nature arising from public actions of a legislative or political character, but one of the most serious aspects of the present-day uncertainty and insecurity, felt not only by the young but principally by them, is the limitation imposed by the development of our social pattern upon their system of choice of activity and employment. I spoke a short while back about the falling off in the numbers of newspapers and the near impossibility of establishing a new newspaper, how sad this was and what unfortunate consequences it had on freedom as we understand it. The same is true, or nearly true, of other vital media of communication. The British Broadcasting Corporation is a great organization which can pride itself upon achievements of world stature, but it has been devised on monolithic lines as one single corporation, and recent attempts to create even minor corporations for secondary broadcasting purposes were unhappily defeated. The desire to see other corporations is not unfriendliness to the BBC, or a failure to recognize what it has contributed to the culture, entertainment, and education of this country. It is a recognition that, in a healthy society, choice of employment must be a vital feature. To have a single employer for this vast range of broadcasting activity is socially undesirable and a restraint on freedom of employment. It is true that the restriction may be more theoretical than real, but if it exists in the mind of a person unable to find employment in the BBC and having no alternative public corporation engaged in similar activities to which to appeal, it is as real as if the facts indeed confirmed it.

The situation is, of course, improved by the Independent Television circuits and the multiplicity of contractors, but their multiplicity is on a geographical basis. There is one only for each area. Whatever the merits or demerits of increasing the volume of broadcasting – and the arguments against it at this moment must be formidable – there can be no opinions about the merits of increasing the range of employment and of employers, and one would hope that this factor will be much in the minds of those persons responsible for reshaping broadcasting policy when the time comes.

But it is not only in public matters that these restrictions exist. It is a sad commentary on our affairs today that, while splendid appointments boards exist within universities, and are available to other young people after training, the one suggestion that can and will never be made to them is that they should set up on their own. They will be offered a choice of public employment in the civil service, the diplomatic corps, of employment in great industries, of employment in a large number of substantial corporations where they can work their way up, if sufficiently talented and fortunate, to positions of authority and power, and might become members of the mystical establishment; but they are offered at all times a certainty of working for other people. No one today would be advised that it was possible to open a bicycle factory or a tyre factory or a sausage factory, that with safety he could even open a tobacco kiosk or a small groceries shop. The ostensible protections of the public in the way of the abolition of retail price maintenance may well have sounded the death knell of the small trader.

We live in a world regulated by massive cartels and corporations. Their undeviating benevolence and social virtue cannot conceal their character as lifeless and spiritless in relation to the free individual. We live in a world where he cannot take flight to a tent on the hills, even if he procures planning consent, for the need to make a livelihood dominates all other considerations to a point far beyond its relevance in previous generations, and precisely for the reasons that I have indicated. Nor is the liberty of an individual in vital matters necessarily safeguarded if he submits to corporate employment. The amalgamation of the takeover bid, beneficent as it may be in commercial, corporate and industrial terms, is nevertheless a real invasion of personal choice of employment. Quite recently in a free society some 70,000 people found themselves transferred by a board-room decision from the employment of one company to the employment of another for which they had never opted. The other company may be as good and better than their original employer, but should changes of this magnitude be effected by a board-room decision, even if mildly recommended by government intervention?

In the Communist countries the citizen knows that the political principles under which he is living consciously and deliberately trammel and curtail his liberty. In a free democratic state, such as we believe ourselves to live in, it is the unperceived and unconscious intrusion of authoritative notes which must create an atmosphere of profound discontent. Such matters belong to the science of government, but the science of government, however closely and carefully investigated in the universities, proceeds piecemeal and *per saltum* in its actual practice in the workshops of democratic society.

It may be that these observations will be regarded as the dyspeptic afterthoughts of near senility, that those robust and young enough would see no challenge or threat in them, and take them in their stride as the everyday manifestations of human life. I hope so, but I doubt so. For the problem we are confronted with is really the problem of the ambit of government, for what purpose government exists and to what ends it should be directed. Governmental enthusiasm can be more dangerous than lassitude and insolence where it works in isolation and without a given direction and a given plan. One could multiply *ad infinitum* the instances of undue paternalism and seemingly unwarranted interference in private life by well-meaning governments. Spasmodic regard is paid to our health. We are urged not to smoke cigarettes – very properly, since all information should be available. We are prevented by regulation from having that quality demonstrated to us on television but not in the papers. In my early youth I thought I had lost touch with the vocative case after early classical conjugations, but it enjoys a new and unwelcome lease of life. Every morning a benevolent authority directs me to drink a pint of milk, to go to work on an egg – admonitions arising from a warmth of heart but nevertheless they send a slight chill down the spine. No great harm comes of them, but they are redolent of a society which is determined to tell all its members what they ought or ought not to do and to regard the exercise of personal liberty and discretion as an unwanted eccentricity.

Perhaps the best or worst illustration of the most recent trends towards extreme paternalism and domestic interference is to be found in the newly proposed domestic legislation, the Divorce Reform Bill. This in many respects is an admirable measure, insofar as it brings the prospect of liberation from intolerable matrimonial bonds to many people upon whom much misery is inflicted by preserving an appearance without a reality. But the price that has had to be paid to seek to procure support for this Bill is an unwelcome one, for in theory the Bill replaces tht present doctrine of the matrimonial offence – whereby a marriage is dissoluble if one party commits adultery, deserts the other, inflicts cruelty upon the other or behaves in some other intolerable fashion – for a comprehensive doctrine that the sole ground for divorce is that the marriage has irretrievably broken down. It is true indeed that when examined this is to be regarded, and the draftsmen clearly hope that it will be, as a formality, but it is the enshrined principle upon which the Bill is founded; and although normally the establishment of a matrimonial offence is to be regarded as proof that the marriage has broken down irretrievably, nevertheless there is reserved to the court a right to refuse a divorce if it is not satisfied, on the evidence, that the marriage has broken down irretrievably. I shall vote for this measure if the occasion arises, because of its overall benefits, but I cannot view, without deep concern, the notion that it is the business of any public official or public body or government to investigate in detail the most intimate of all human relationships, and that any government should be entitled to scrutinize for the purpose of a divorce law the whole of the subjective human relationship, and require it to be exposed in detail for such scrutiny even if this is maintained to be a theoretical possibility alone.

We could not have a more dramatic demonstration of how far we have gone in assuming responsibility for the lives of other people which they have not sought to introduce to us.

I have in these observations selected at random, and seemingly in disjointed fashion, a few instances of matters which in my view encroach on liberty where previously there was no such encroachment, or not such gross encroachment. I believe that they add up to a code of conduct on our part which is not in the best interests of human society.

Parliamentary government in the form which we enjoy it is

long-winded, pompous, ritualistic and in many ways open to criticism as being out of touch with the age in which we live. But it has a supreme merit in that, over the centuries, it has evolved a system which can, if operated by men of determination and courage, protect the liberties of the people for whom it works. But if a democratic legislature does not protect liberty it serves no purpose. That fundamental requirement is the justification for all its anomalies and anachronisms, a sufficient justification, without which other more efficient systems could be designed to do the job as well and better. We do not want any such systems because we want to preserve our liberties. The essential features within the parliamentary machine for the preservation of liberty are the opportunity for reflection and the opportunity for protest. Hence if the machine operates helter-skelter one of these essentials is destroyed.

Let us willingly accept all the weariness associated with the system of government that contains these vital safeguards. Let us be wary indeed to tolerate any excuses for abandoning them even in isolated instances.

('Thank-Offering to Britain Fund' Lecture, March 27, 1968)

2. *Takeovers and the Employee*

The time has come – and not a moment too soon – to ask whether the cult of the shareholder has not gone too far.

Shareholder worship reached its highest peak in 1962 at the time of the Jenkins Committee of Enquiry into the whole system of company law, when it was only by a whisker that the legality of a non-voting share was retained. Moreover, despite the refusal to ostracize the share in law, it has assumed a wholly disreputable air in City and financial circles and particularly with institutional investors.

On all sides the feeling has, up till now, prevailed that the destinies of a company must, in the ultimate analysis, be controlled by its shareholders. This ethos is now proclaimed daily from the temples of the financial High Priests. Any contrary view is sacrilege. But it is necessary to examine the logic and morality of the proposition and, more important, its consequences, and to inquire whether we can continue to operate a sensible financial and industrial system if the principle of shareholder control is relentlessly maintained.

First, as to its morality. A shareholder is a worthy individual. Most of them have placed sums of money for investment in business organizations created and operated by other people. The great preponderance of shareholders know almost nothing of the businesses which have their financial support. They enter them on the advice of stockbrokers or bankers; they forsake them on the same advice and without a tear or whisper of regret.

Most shareholders today flit from investment to investment, and the impersonality of the picture is accentuated by the development of the unit trust where the shareholder no longer even makes an individual choice of any particular business or trade, but decides to participate in a minute share of a share held on his behalf by another impersonal organization. In the main, the personal interest or participation of shareholders in their companies is a convenient fiction to preserve the doctrine of shareholders' control, and the doctrine has become associated with an elaborate code, carefully distilled, and of real moral content, whereby a good shareholder is a shareholder who is moved only by considerations of monetary benefit.

Any decision relating to the share must be judged solely by its value in financial terms. Any offer for the share is a good offer if it produces more money for the shareholder than its alternative. Moreover it is unsporting, and even alleged to be a breach of the takeover code, if a shareholder allows himself to be moved by more altruistic considerations, and thereby prevents another shareholder from pursuing his honourably selfish motives. There has, indeed, been some criticism of the egotistical shareholders of the *News of the World*, who improperly refused to accept a larger bid of money out of mere considerations of loyalty and long-time association.

But the vice of this matter is not in relation to the shareholders and their ability or inability to make profits, but in the national damage that ensues. The question is whether this weird financial code may not do irreparable injury to large areas of the nation's industry and commerce. Is it sensible that the only consideration that should weigh before a change of ownership and control of an important industry, possibly producing a vital public service, should be the decision of the shareholder alone, motivated solely by considerations of price?

There can hardly be a publicly-quoted company in the country which could not find its ownership transferred to another company, not even necessarily larger or richer, and the decision reached without consultation with employees. The servants of the company are often more numerous than its shareholders. Their stake in the company is demonstrably more important to them than is the investment to the shareholder. But their employer can be changed without reference to them, without their approval, and without regard to the consequences upon them, including loss of employment. If the paramount objective was one of efficiency and of economy there might indeed be arguments that a change of this sort should be permitted, but there is no evidence that in most cases efficiency or economy are factors that are germane to the transfer of ownership, which is unashamedly inspired by profit motivation. If, as admittedly happens, greater efficiency and economy do result, this is not a certain but a chance and incidental result. That one man should have his job and security imperilled to make another man richer is a distasteful notion in a modern society, without taking into account the public interest.

There is no impartial arbiter to decide the effect of the change on the industry concerned, the effect on prices, on commodities or services and – subject to the limited and rather toothless protection of the Monopolies Commission – to decide the likely increase or reduction of competition. The decision is arrived at without consultation with customers, suppliers, persons engaged in allied or service trades, or with a myriad other interests which may add up in financial and emotional content to a great deal more than the value of the shareholding.

Admittedly, nobody wishes to see a multiplication of government controls, and the mere notion of an increase of the Civil Service to regulate takeover bids leaves a predisposition to feel that the present situation, however bad, could only be made worse by further attempts at governmental regulation. With the government machine struggling to digest the immense tasks of surveillance and control which have been undertaken by this and previous administrations, a scientific attempt to regulate the transfer of ownership of industry is plainly impossible and probably undesirable. But this does not mean that something effective cannot be done by self-help.

In an article of this length it is only possible to pose the problems. I doubt if many thinking people would regard the continuation of the present takeover antics, and the uncontrolled right for any bidder to acquire any industry at his whim by dint of creating additional shareholding within his own company, as a sensible working policy. Nor, irrespective of political views, would they regard it as fair that the only interests to be consulted are those of shareholders whose associations are often as tenuous as I have indicated, and for whom the law had carefully contrived that their investment should involve no legal liability in the way of personal risk or obligation.

There are some possible solutions – and all need a careful and even suspicious approach. First, whether safeguards should not now be provided for the private companies and partnerships which, because of the future incidence of estate duty and other fiscal burdens, need to have a public quotation to provide a sufficient liquidity of assets to their present owners. It is ironic that, for some years since the end of the Second World War, the trend towards public quotation was largely prompted by a desire to preserve companies which, without it, would have been threatened by sale out of family ownership or control, for estate duty or similar reason, and this tendency has been further encouraged by tax provisions such as the surtax direction and the closed company provisions, which put a privately owned company or a company under closed control at a marked disadvantage.

Today, however, if the companies shake off these disadvantages by introducing an element of public ownership, they now – unless the original owners retain something over 50 per cent of the voting shareholding – expose themselves to the predatory eyes of the takeover kings. And, with the emphasis on disclosure, even by small private companies, which was a feature of the last Companies Act, the task of those wishing to acquire their neighbours has been made that much easier by the existence of useful balance sheet information conveniently filed at a public registry.

The measures that I believe should be urgently examined are four:

1 The reinstatement in status of the non-voting share, and particularly a more considered analysis of the objections which were mounted against it on highly specialized 'City' grounds. A strong case can be made out for enabling a man to introduce capital into his business without giving up the essential rights of control so far as the trading aspects of the business are concerned. But the strength of the contrary case must not be discounted.

2 To restore the status of the exempt private company, and to free it from the discriminatory legislation that drives successful private companies into public ownership.

3 To introduce more effective City controls on the creation of any utilization of new share capital for the acquisition of companies outside the business character of the acquiring company.

4 Possibly, although here one must tread warily, to introduce a Board of Trade panel whose consent must be forthcoming for any bid to acquire a business over a certain size. If such a panel were introduced, it would be my view that it should be asked to consider the simple and solitary question (often, however, involving a difficult answer) of whether the proposed takeover is in the public interest – or at least that the applicant should discharge the lower onus of showing that it is not contrary to the public interest. Public interest would include the fate of the employees to be balanced against other relevant national considerations.

I do not believe that this is a problem that can be resolved by improved takeover codes or even by looking across the Atlantic for guidance from the American SEC. I believe that any solution requires the firm recognition that the issues involved transcend the interest of shareholders as shareholders, and that, virtuous as they may be as a class, our devotion to their interests regardless of other factors is misguided and damaging to the national picture.

It would be unfair not to recognize that some attempt has been made to deal with this problem by such devices as the IRC and the Monopolies Commission. But these two bodies have unavoidable conflicting policies and between them cover only a small edge of the problem.

The device of the joint stock company has long been regarded as one of the glories of the common law – developed and refined to the highest degree in this and other Commonwealth countries and in the USA. It would be tragic if a device to which we owe a great part of our financial structure, our Stock Exchange, our investment system, the possibility for people of moderate means to participate in great industrial adventures, were at the end of the day to redound to the public detriment.

(*Sunday Times*, January 12, 1969)

3. *A Plea for the Small Business*

In a recent lecture I used the phrase 'social claustrophobia' to suggest a malaise which I thought affected a number of young people today, the sense that society was closing in on them. I instanced as one symptom that, in the selection of employment, there was a tacit assumption that no youngster could today start a business for himself. In short, that his unalterable destiny was to take service for life under one master or another.

The principle of self-employment has, of course, not been totally eroded. It still retains some relevance in the professions, although with nationalised medicine and much larger partnership conceptions amongst accountants, solicitors, architects and other professional practitioners, the wholly independent freelance is becoming an anachronism. He survives almost exclusively – and by no means without problems – at the Bar and in a few other fields of limited manpower, such as piano tuning.

I recently carried out a private and unscientific Gallup Poll amongst some leading industrialist friends. My question was whether, in their opinion, and in their own or related industries, it was still possible for a young man after suitable training to start a business of his own with any prospect of success. Although the replies were not wholly discouraging – some thought, for instance, that there were areas in the manufacture of components and accessories where with skilful selection opportunity still existed – they were unanimous that the choice of such a career would be hazardous and eccentric.

The capital required on every estimate was daunting and, even if the capital for factory, machinery, and initial running costs were available, the amounts now needed for a proper distribution organization, for securing export markets and, if any retail element was involved, for advertising, took the matter clean out of the realms of practical possibility. It was still theoretically possible to open a shop, but even here the range was limited. You might, it was thought, if you were a trained pharmacist, but would find yourself at a disadvantage in bulk purchasing since many suppliers gave special discounts. A grocery shop was regarded as quite impossible, and particularly so since the abolition of retail price maintenance. For some reason my tobacconist tycoon thought that you could open a tobacco kiosk but that your margins of profit would be slight, and he recommended a regimen of two meals a day. Antique shops and boutiques remain the easiest, but were pullulating at such a rate that the more recent arrivals would be lucky to share a customer between them.

Nor is the climate a healthy one with the established small or private business even where it is holding its own against its larger neighbours. No student of government since the First World War can find firm signs of any social or economic policy directed to particular economic sectors. It is therefore unkind (and unduly flattering) to suspect that the successive pieces of legislation discouraging, and even destructive of, small business enterprises were a part of any deliberate policy. But their existence is undeniable. The elaborate surtax provisions penalizing private companies under the control of five persons or fewer drove a successful private company – even of a modest scale – to seek public quotation or to expand its ownership so as to avoid the crippling obligation to clear out each year's kitty. The newer 'close company' provisions which have replaced the surtax provisions are, in some ways, even more restrictive.

Again it would seem the intention to drive small units into public or wider ownership, as though the maintenance and control of a small entity in a few hands was to be reprobated. Moreover, in other directions company law has made a set against the small or private company. The abolition of the 'exempt private company' was a piece of discriminatory legislation, justified by the arguable precept that disclosure of a company's affairs had a virtue of its own, even where no case was made out for any third person's right to possess the information so disclosed. In the event, small businesses are now obliged to publish their balance sheets and to disclose details of their trading and other matters of valued privacy to great trading rivals who must find the availability of this information most useful in any plan to gobble them up.

It is difficult to find throughout the legislation programmes of the last twenty-five years any measure sympathetic to the small business or the small company, and the *coup de grace* is nearly always administered by the operation of estate duty. If the shares in a private company remain in individual control and the company assumes a value of even £100,000, an extremely modest present-day valuation, the estate duty to be paid on the death of the sole shareholder would be £50,000 in respect of the company alone. Inevitably the unfortunate owner – if provident – must look around before his death either to enlarge the ownership of his company or to sell his business to some bigger organization.

This is not the place to argue the merits or demerits of small as opposed to large businesses. We are today preoccupied to a point of obsession with the reorganization of industry on a massive scale. Much of what is being done is undoubtedly sound and praiseworthy. Much of what is being done or proposed to be done requires, in my opinion, second thoughts. The cry has gone out that we must contrive to compete in the export market on competitive terms. To do so is undoubtedly a desideratum of the first order, but it should not blind us to all other considerations. So the total destruction of the small business and the opportunity for sturdy individualism in its establishment should not be regarded as a tolerable consequence of export efficiency. We should settle for a decimal point of lower efficiency and the salving of some small business to give us a more balanced social picture.

It is, I believe, very necessary to remember that we have been the leading architects and sponsors of a mixed economy, and that a mixed economy requires opportunities for business big and small. Today the young cannot, except in the rarest instances, start their own businesses; cannot be their own masters, and must in the ordinary way accept an ordered scheme of employment from cradle to grave. The spirit of venture and audacity associated with being young and remaining on your own is at a premium, and is in danger of being priced out of the market. Its disappearance would involve a serious loss to a country which has for many years placed much dependence on them.

The problem is a big one. It needs more serious review by people better equipped than I am in the fields of politics and economics, but it seems to me there are some steps that can be taken without great cost and without great difficulty. I would venture to recommend the following measures for consideration as being designed to encourage the restoration of the lost art of fending for yourself.

First and foremost I should like to see introduced an estate duty scheme which enables the repayment of estate duty over a very extended period where an undertaking is given that a business will be retained in private control. It is already possible to compromise with the Estate Duty Office if you undertake to retain in your possession a work of art of national importance. It seems to me that a similar indulgence for a small business would be appropriate.

Equally, I think that the exempt private company should be reinstated so that the small business does not need to disclose information about its trading to the world at large. The Inland Revenue and public officials are already entitled to any information they require. The notion that the filing of balance sheets is a protection to creditors is based on the fallacy that any such balance sheet would be sufficiently current to be relevant. A creditor who needs information about a company can indulge in a little self-help by asking for it before he extends the credit; but it is, in my view, of considerable importance that small companies should be protected from damaging disclosures which are of no benefit to the public at large, but which can be very detrimental to them.

The close company provisions should be altered so that they no longer operate as coercive of wider ownership. An obligation to distribute a reasonable measure of profit is plainly necessary, but can operate without having special relevance to the number of people controlling the company.

The battle of retail price maintenance has been fought out. It would appear to have established very firmly that its abolition was for the benefit of the public at large, justifying any consequences to the individual small shopkeeper or wholesaler; but we must recognize that in the retail trades we have made it unlikely that small-holding will remain a continuing feature of our natural life. Believing, as I do, that efficiency is only one factor in the scheme of human affairs, and that human happiness rates higher than human competence, I retain the hope that we shall continue to look with kindliness and sympathy on the efforts by private individuals to retain small businesses in their own hands, and where appropriate to pass them on from generation to generation.

(*Sunday Telegraph*, May 25, 1969)

4. *Abolition of the Death Penalty*

This is a debate of great importance. A variety of viewpoints have been expressed, but until now I had not heard the viewpoint so enthusiastically and atavistically expressed as it was by the noble Lord, Lord Molson. I have the deepest respect for the noble Lord, Lord Molson; he is a very humane man. But I cannot help thinking that the arguments which he advanced in this matter are not, for once, helpful to our deliberations, and it is unusual that his arguments should not be helpful.

As I understand him, he made two points: one was that he has a moral position, just as the abolitionists have a moral position. I should prefer to refrain from any moral position in this matter. I am not quite sure what sort of moral position it is that is maintained by a sense of retribution, a determination that somebody should suffer because he has committed a crime. It seems to me that this takes into regard only the crime and not the criminal. It discards entirely all the careful examination of the circumstances of the crime that we now regard as indispensable, and regarded as indispensable when we had hanging. We reviewed with great care the background of the criminal, the circumstances in which he came to commit the crime, and a number of other factors that were so highly relevant that the whole element of retribution in this matter could have no further part in a civilized consideration of the question.

The other matter raised by the noble Lord was the question of public opinion. This, I think, has featured in a number of the speeches we have heard today. It is apparently suggested that it is possible to gauge public opinion on this matter and to derive some benefit from the communal view. I believe this to be a totally impossible and irrelevant proposition. I do not think – and I speak, I believe, as a sincere democrat, as sincere as anyone here – that public opinion has the slightest relevance. I say this unapologetically and unhesitatingly. When we wanted to review this matter very carefully – and I think the most elaborate review of it was undoubtedly the Royal Commission which reported in 1953 – after four years we assembled a number of extremely expert people who reviewed evidence over that period. They travelled in a variety of foreign countries, they heard innumerable witnesses, they studied the subject as closely and meticulously as conscientious human beings can, and they arrived at a conclusion.

It is important to remember that they were debarred from recommending the abolition of capital punishment. That was excluded from their terms of reference. They had therefore to consider whether the operation of the death penalty should be limited. Abolition was not a course which it was open to them to recommend. They have after years of deliberation arrived at a particular conclusion on an informed basis. How can we suggest that a task fulfilled by these people after those exertions can be passed on to the whole community? Nor would the community thank us for it. This is a specialized matter of penology. It deserves to be dealt with by specialists. It is entirely avoiding the difficult issue to pretend that you can make some appeal to an electorate on a question of this kind. I think it is dodging our own responsibility to assume that there is an electoral voice that can have any relevance in regard to a matter of this kind.

There is another question. It appears to be regarded in some quarters as rather tactless and indelicate to indicate the nature of the matter we are discussing. I think it was the noble Lord, Lord Salter, who said that he hoped we would not talk about hanging. I am afraid we must talk about hanging, because hanging is the operation with which we are concerned. If your Lordships read the Gowers Report, you will find that the Royal Commission carefully considered the possibility of any alternative and arrived at the considered conclusion that there were no alternatives at that stage. They considered the gas chamber; they considered the electric chair; they considered the possibility of injections of some form or another, and they arrived still at the conclusion that the only thing that we could do was to hang people. It is therefore hanging that we are dealing with. However squeamish we may be about it, however reluctant we may be to face up to the fact that it is this hideous human operation with which we are concerned. To drive the point home, I should like to draw attention to some of the matters that this unfortunate Commission had to consider as an inevitable consequence of retaining this abominable practice. I have no wish to harrow anyone, but I do not think we should engage in a debate of this kind unless we are prepared to consider the details. None of them are especially harrowing, and here are some of them:

> Prisoners under sentence of death should be allowed to listen to the wireless, subject to any conditions that the authorities may prescribe.
> The rule should be maintained that prison officers may not smoke on duty in the condemned cell.

The provision of sedatives for prisoners during their stay in the condemned cell, and in particular immediately before execution, must lie within the discretion of the prison medical officer.

There are innumerable hideous details of this kind with which this wretched Commission had to deal.

How obvious it is that if we can once and for all discard this appalling practice we must do so with an enthusiasm unequalled by any step we have taken in this House. But, of course, we must do so only if we are convinced that it is right to do so, and at the same time safeguard the public interest. But certain it is that we should know what it is we are talking about.

There are two matters with which we are concerned at the moment: one is the preliminary matter about whether we have sufficient information. In my view, any one of your Lordships who has read the Gowers Report is seized of all the information he can possibly require on this matter; I do not believe that there is any information that can usefully be added. It appears to me to be absolutely nonsensical – and I use the word deliberately – to suggest that there would be added a relevant amount of material to that corpus of knowledge by an additional few months of investigation. It is absolute nonsense; there is no other word to be used in respect of it, and therefore I use the word, because in a matter of this importance I think the right words ought to be used.

There is another consideration. I believe that it is vitally urgent that we dispose of hanging, because until we abolish capital punishment we shall not derive the benefit of the abolition of capital punishment. I believe that the twilight period gives us the worst of both possible worlds. I think the neurotic and neurasthenic atmosphere that prevails leads many criminals to believe that they are escaping the gallows because this is the transitional era. I think that when we have abolished hanging we shall then be able to know what the final effects are likely to be. Until we have abolished it, I am absolutely convinced that all the statistics will be irrelevant.

There is another matter. We are told that we need six months, five months, four months in this period of time to add additional relevant statistics. But is this a relevant period of time? Is it a characteristic period of time? We must remember that we have injected into society in the last few years a desperate set of new criminals. We are enjoying an abundance of gambling in this country unequalled previously in its history. This has produced a mass of criminals of unprecedented activity, vigour and determination. They can be removed by sensible legislation by this House and elsewhere, but at this moment they are here and they are rendering any kind of test, any kind of standard, quite unrepresentative. I cannot see how we can possibly pretend that this moment is a representative moment of time in which to take a test. It is quite remarkable, if I may venture to say so, that we have had so little increase in murder during this particular period. It seems to me clear on the face of it that the experiment has stood the test, the most exacting test that it could possibly receive. It has stood the test of a period of time when determined criminals are operating under conditions that did not exist before.

We must remember that the type of criminal with whom we are now dealing is not one deterred by prospects of punishment. He is a criminal who believes that he has acquired wealth and influence in society that will save him from any sort of punishment. Many of these criminals, we know, formed the view – and apparently formed it with sufficient validity for us to alter the time-honoured principle of unanimity of jury verdicts – that they can tamper with juries. These were not people worried by the prospect of being hanged. These were people firmly convinced that they had their fates in their own purses. This is demonstrated by an inspection of the same sort of situation in the United States of America. If you look at America and observe the activities of the Al Capones, who mowed down men in the notorious Valentine Day murders in a state where capital punishment was retained, he was not worried about the prospect of going to the electric chair. He knew that he had the lawyers and the judges and the senators and everyone else who was determining his fate safely in his pocket.

What is required to safeguard the community is not the retention of an abominable anachronism but a certainty of conviction; that is what is required. And we shall not be doing the police force any service, by procuring the retention of this penalty. Hideous penalties produce hideous social conditions. When people say, as

Lord Molson said, that we must not interfere with a penalty which expresses the righteous sense of indignation of the multitude, what would he have said two hundred years ago when people were being hanged for theft? Would he have said that we must not interfere with the hanging of people for theft because this expresses the righteous indignation of the multitude? When howling mobs were watching people being hanged, drawn and quartered, would it not have been an unjustifiable interference in the sense of righteous indignation of the multitude to make any change in this practice?

I think this is an extremely difficult question. I think it falls to be dealt with by people who have made a detailed study of the subject. I think this House contains a unique collection of people who have made such a study. I do not think we need make any appeal to outside knowledge, to democratic decision.

I think that we ought to disregard entirely the political implications. Apparently for some reason a number of people's feathers are out of place because it is felt that bringing the debate on at this moment is a convenience to the Government. May I say that, speaking from these Benches, I am astronomically indifferent to the convenience of the Government. I think the Government will accept that without hesitation. But I do not for one moment see why, because we believe that the Government may be convenienced by this, we should regard that as an argument for not dealing seriously with the issue. Unless the suggestion that they are being convenienced interferes in some way with the validity of the argument and the relevance of the considerations, it should be dismissed entirely from all our minds.

A much more logical course was adopted by the Opposition in the other place; it was perfectly logical to seek to pass a vote of censure. It is totally illogical to seek to postpone the decision for several months, and I hope I shall not be accused of making a debating point if I point out that it is a little odd that in the other place the Leader of the Opposition Party should not have regarded himself as precluded from making a final decision by any absence of information, when now we are informed, with great emphasis, that they cannot make their decision because they have not the information. Mr. Heath, and a great many other people, who are very responsible people and make decisions on a very responsible basis, found it possible to reach that decision yesterday, without waiting for the additional four months.

I would conclude only by saying this. Almost all the young people with whom I talk regard the retention of capital punishment as some sort of peculiar whim on the part of elder folk, who clearly must have some sexual interest in the matter. I have found absolute horror on the part of the young with whom I have consulted over the notion that this type of penalty should be preserved in their society. And remember, please, that it is their society we are making.

(Speech in the House of Lords, December 17, 1969)

5. *Student Participation in Higher Education*

We could talk at great length about why students are unhappy. I think the answer is a simple one: they are unhappy because they sense a shape and form of society that they do not find entirely satisfactory to themselves. That is hardly surprising. This is an enormous theme. But I think it is unrealistic not to accept that the shape of our society today would be discouraging to older, more robust, more experienced people than students. If, therefore, we encounter manifestations of unhappiness and uncertainty, then those who have shaped society and have the continuing responsibility for doing so should accept a large measure of the blame and must not try to assign it to the unfortunate persons who are expressing their anxiety, unhappiness and discontent.

But for a student who came here today, and who might be in the public galleries, I think he or she will have found it rather a disappointing experience because of the extraordinary reasonableness of the speeches made by all noble Lords. That must be profoundly frustrating to someone who was hoping to hear expressed the ordinary conventional reaction of the older generation. I would advise students who place trust on the words spoken here not to attach too great an importance to them; because I am not sure that very much has emerged in the way of tangible promises or benefits.

We have heard a number of distinguished educationists. Nearly all of them have spoken with great approbation of the principle of student participation. I hope that I may utter a word of calculated reaction. I do not attach enormous importance to student participation. This I do not think is a subject of very great importance at all. I know that one speaker, I think it was the noble Lord, Lord Beaumont of Whitley, who spoke earlier, seemed to regard it as the millennium. He seemed to think that the moment we had full-scale student participation, all the university problems would be solved. For my part, I would afford full-scale participation far more freely and willingly than any speaker I have heard today; but I should expect very little to emerge from it. I do not think it would solve any problems. I think the student participators would in the end wish to withdraw from participation as being rather wasteful of their time. I think it would be exciting and novel, and it may be even constructive in certain fields, for them to participate, but the idea that you are going to re-shape the universities because a number of young people are invited to sit in council with their elders, without going into the whole question of the policies that are to be considered and the reasons that are to be considered and the road that you are taking, seems to me to be fanciful nonsense.

Therefore my position is a simple one. I would not hesitate for a moment – as I was sorry to see Lord James hesitate – in having students sitting in committees even on matters as revered and sacred as the pay of lecturers. I do not see why students should not participate in discussions on that subject. I should not leave the students to have the ultimate decision in the matter or give them a preponderance of votes, for obvious reasons; but it is perfectly acceptable that a student can be seated at the table and air his views as to whether a particular lecturer is worthy of a particular increase of pay. If there are others who say that although the lecturer does not lecture very well he is an immense authority on

Greek adverbs, and therefore he ought to receive higher pay on that account, then their views could prevail, the views of the student having been heard.

I believe that a rather half-hearted offer of student participation is likely to create a notion of hypocrisy and humbug. I think the offer should be made unconditionally and wholeheartedly. But we should recognize that it means little more than a token, and that it is not going to resolve the extremely deep and difficult problems that exist in the universities and are a reflection of the problems which exist in our society today. Those problems are not to be solved by student participation or by the participation of any other section of the community. They would not be solved even by lawyers' participation; they would not be solved by the participation of clerics or by the participation of any section of the community, because they are deep social problems that have to be solved by social discoveries on our part.

We are enormously concerned in talking about students as a community. I agreed with the right reverend Prelate when he said that this is rather a dangerous form of language to use. Also I think it is a slight absurdity. I do not think that students are a community in the sense that one should expect a whole group of people to line up on a particular issue because they are a particular age group and because they inhabit a specific number of buildings in particular areas. I cannot think of any social problem of difficulty on which a group of students asked to express their opinion would themselves be unanimous. I cannot think of any social problem of difficulty on which a group of students united with a group of older people in one room would divide, with the students on one side and the older people on the other. That is unrealistic and false. Difficult problems need to be solved by the decisions of wise people of all ages, whether they be students or anyone else.

That brings me to the final matter to which I wish to invite your Lordships' and, if I may venture to say so, the students' consideration. The purpose of all education, the purpose of all this, is not to produce people with degrees; not to produce people who have professional or other qualifications, but to produce civilized human beings. In my view the controversy that is said to have been raging has been greatly exaggerated, and I think that one of the values of today's debate has been to hear distinguished educationists telling us that both the problems and the suggestion of student unrest have been exaggerated; and that the difficulties and problems of environment and so forth are not to be found as a wide-scale manifestation. I think this needs to be said, and said loudly. But in the controversy enough has emerged to make clear that some students are forgetting that it is more important to be civilized human beings than to be effective members of the student body. Some things are happening within the student world that makes it necessary, I think, to invite them to stop and reflect about the essential values of human behaviour.

When one reads that students burst into the rooms of their tutors and steal documents; when one reads that students are assaulting their lecturers; when one reads that students are conducting campaigns (and I saw one of unparalleled vilification) against their teachers, in terms which would make Titus Oates drool with envy, one wonders whether they have a real sense of the issues involved; whether it is so important to have a say in the curriculum; whether it is not more important to realize that these things are the ultimate enormities and that even if you leave the university without a degree, even if you have some doubts about the excellence of the curriculum, it is better to have had inculcated in you those principles of reasonable and decent behaviour that will make you acceptable to society as a whole.

In short, my Lords, if principles of partnership are to prevail, let us try to emphasize to the students that we want acceptable partners. They tax us with all sorts of inadequacies. Let us not for once hesitate to tax them with a few inadequacies and say that if they are to enter into a fruitful partnership, they must learn to behave as we would hope to behave. This has nothing to do with student participation, but it has to do with behaviour of human beings; and it has, I think, much to do with the future of this country as a nation.

(Speech in the House of Lords, April 23, 1969)

6. Race Relations in Britain

I do not know whether the noble Lord, Lord O'Hagan, is justified in saying that there has been a serious deterioration in race relations because of a few people who have made unseemly and inappropriate observations calculated, perhaps deliberately calculated – one cannot be sure – to exacerbate the situation. I am inclined to think that on the whole the amount of publicity they have received exceeds their importance or their lasting significance. That is my own belief. But I do not think that anyone could deprecate or deplore too strongly any observations calculated to arouse misgivings on the part of any section of the community that people were concerned to bring up a feeling of hate and resentment against them. I know of no higher crime that a man can commit against his neighbour than that he should make him feel that sections of the community living round him hate him, resent him and may wish to do him injury. If that could be instilled in the minds of the people concerned, perhaps for political motivation, if they could realize the extreme enormity of what they were doing, without perhaps having in mind that they were committing a crime of such magnitude. I am sure that that crime would be committed less often and in far less extreme manner.

I do not think that the Press, on the whole, has been too bad. If you review the Press you find a fairly even, a fairly responsible, a fairly just and a fairly tolerant approach to this matter. I have seen features in the newspapers that I have deplored and thought to be wrong, but on the whole I have not thought that the Press has done badly. What the Press does do, and what I think is often very wrong, is to call up illustrations from other countries and warn us of the dangers that exist and which we can find if we examine the history and folklore of some other place. Nearly always it is totally inappropriate, and nearly always they relate to our friends in the United States of America.

If I may venture to say so, it is great nonsense to find any parallel at all between this problem in the United States and the problems of our coloured immigrants in this country; because in the United States of America there is, unhappily, an established history of the most unfortunate and often the most prejudiced and the most difficult character. We have no such history. We are not saddled with this kind of legacy. We have not the problems of the Southern States, of lynching, of the Scottsboro cases and matters that are bound to remain in the minds of the coloured population in that country for generations. We are in the fortunate position of starting from scratch. We have none of those matters to prejudice the position, to ruffle the surface, to make it more difficult for us to build sensible and reasonable institutions with people living side by side as civilized neighbours.

I think it is very wrong to call up these foreign illustrations. It is particularly wrong because nobody ever calls up illustrations from countries which have no such problems. No one ever calls attention to the fact that, for instance, apart from individual political matters, on the whole in France this problem has never been of serious significance for years, for generations, for centuries. It is always to a problem based on conditions where no parallel of any kind exists that our attention is directed and solemn warnings are uttered. I think it is time that we pointed out that people who are calling up the customs of other countries ought to have an intimate knowledge of those countries; and they ought also to have an intimate knowledge of their own country before they make these false and invalid comparisons.

(Speech in the House of Lords, July 16, 1969)

7. Divorce Reform

I have had a good deal of experience over the years as a lawyer who occasionally practised in the field of divorce. It is a disagreeable field, and as one became relatively more successful one readily discarded it. It is not a field in which many lawyers are very anxious to practise, if they can avoid it.

My enthusiasm about this Bill, about which I have many criticisms, is that it makes the divorce law more seemly and more respectable and it takes some of the disagreeable and unsavoury elements out of the existing law. It is for that reason that I commend it to your Lordships. I should not wish to presume to impose on anyone my own view on matters of conscience. People who conscientiously believe that it is wrong to increase the amount of divorce now in existence, or to make divorce easier, will forbear to vote for the Bill. I would urge upon your Lordships who feel like this, however, to consider whether it is right in those circumstances to impose your conscientious views to the detriment of a number of people who are now suffering a great deal of misery and unhappiness on account of the prevailing conditions in this country under the existing matrimonial law. By all means abstain. It seems to me, however, that this Bill will bring a great deal of relief in many cases of unhappiness. Nor do I believe that it will inflict any of the hardships that have been apprehended by a number of speakers to whom I have listened this evening.

One of my experiences is that a great many women who have been deserted by husbands for a period of five years or longer do not feel strongly about preserving the matrimonial bonds, yet feel a considerable repugnance at taking active steps to dissolve the marriage. Quite often in my office I have had women who have been deserted for a long time by their husbands, and who say, 'What do I have to do?' You say, 'You would have to file a petition and you would have to go into the witness box and give evidence.' They say, 'That I could not do. That is too distasteful.

I should be touching on immensely sensitive areas. I think I will leave matters as they are.'

Many of these marriages are preserved solely on account of inertia; they are not preserved because the prospective petitioner in such a case believes that she is retaining anything of any real value. This Bill will bring relief and assistance in these cases. Many of these women will be quite happy to find that steps are being taken for them which they have an instinctive reluctance and unwillingness to take on their own behalf. I do not suggest that that is the case in relation to every such marriage; nor do I wholly agree that one can say that in all cases it is 'six of one and half a dozen of the other'.

Of course there are many women who late in life are deserted by husbands who ought to know better. There are many cases of women who have made admirable wives and whose husbands discover later in life that a prettier face is more acceptable and who then rationalize themselves into the belief that they are no longer in love with their wife. This is a fact that one must face. But I do not think this is a ground for rejecting the Bill, because the question one has to ask oneself is simply this: what is such a woman retaining? What of value is such a wife retaining after a separation of five years? When a husband has absented himself from the matrimonial home for five years, what is there left of the slightest value, even if it is a case of the gravest injustice and hardship; even if, as is often the case, the woman has been an admirable wife and a great matrimonial wrong has been done to her? What are you depriving her of if you deprive her of the benefit of such a husband?

The noble Lady, Lady Kinloss, made a most moving speech and touched on what was a horrible case. It was a case about which she had received a letter from a wife who was becoming afflicted, or had been afflicted, with arthritis, and whose husband had come to her and said, 'I can no longer remain burdened with an arthritic wife. I want to leave you.' If, in those circumstances, the husband was so callous and so brutal and so devoid of ordinary human sentiment that he would leave his wife, and if he abandoned her for a period of five years, what conceivable hardship would there be to that woman in dissolving that matrimonial union? Nothing but sentiment can remotely pretend that she was in any way damnified by being no longer able to retain the appearance of a marriage in a case as hideous and intolerant as that one. I do not think that is a case that represents any argument against this Bill. With the greatest respect to the noble Lady, I think it represents a most formidable argument in favour of the Bill.

There is another point that I should like to make. We have been told that the greatest area of suffering and unhappiness that needs to be relieved by this Bill is in the case of people who are living apart, because of desertion, normally by a husband, who cannot re-marry but has contracted another union that has every appearance of permanence, and who is anxious to make a home and marriage with a new wife and is prevented from doing so and perhaps has children that he is not able to legitimize. I think that this is a case that needs to be dealt with. It is by no means the only case, however. Under our existing law the most fatal step that a couple can take is to agree to have a separation. Under our present law if a couple agree between themselves, in a civilized and honourable fashion, that the marriage has broken down; that it is intolerable that they should continue to live together, and that it is not in the interests of the children that they should live together, then from that moment onwards it is impossible for them to get a divorce unless one of them is prepared to commit adultery, something which they may have no wish to do. It occurs to me that that is an intolerable situation which will be put right by this Bill, because there is a civilized provision in this Bill which will enable people who have recognized that the marriage has broken down, who have arrived at a civilized arrangement in respect of it, to terminate the marriage by an honourable agreement.

As to the financial provisions, I believe that much has been said that arises from an insufficiently close reading of the Bill by learned lawyers. I think the financial provisions of this Bill, as one might expect from a Bill which has been prepared with every assistance from the Law Commission, are wholly admirable. The financial provisions go as far as it is possible to go. Clause 6 says that in respect of the two new cases of a right to dissolve a marriage – that is to say, where there has been a five-year separation and perhaps what at present we call the 'guilty party' in the marriage takes action: and secondly in a case where there is agreement to dissolve a marriage after a separation of two years (an unlikely case, I may say, for Clause 6 to be invoked, because in such a case the parties would ordinarily have made a part of their agreement the financial arrangements, so that normally Clause 6 will relate to the five-year or longer desertion period where the guilty party can now petition) – no decree nisi is to be made absolute until the court is satisfied that fair, proper and reasonable provisions have been made for the respondent or that the best possible provisions have been made for her.

The suggestion has been aired that we ought to see what further legislation is to emerge before we give this Bill a Second Reading. I can think of no further legislation that can emerge that will add in principle, or even very much in detail, to the provisions of this Bill or will improve it. The judge is given the widest possible discretion: he can make any arrangement he likes under Clause 6 to ensure that a deserted wife is looked after. He can make provision by way of an annual payment; he can make provision by way of a cash settlement; he can make provision by way of a transfer of capital assets. There is no restriction on the type of financial provision that is now available to the judge in relation to these cases. Of course, rules of court will have to be made. There will have to be enlarged indications of the detailed provisions that have been made, but in general terms this Bill says everything that needs to be said.

Clause 4 covers the hardship cases, which it is hypocritical to pretend will not, in certain circumstances, arise. Of course there will be cases where a woman may find herself deprived of a benefit because she has been divorced. A man may provide in a will, or there may be provision in a will where a man's wife is to receive certain benefits on his death. That cannot be duplicated; it cannot be made to read 'his second wife'. You cannot introduce two wives into the one will, and that is a case where obviously a benefit will be lost. Equally, there may be cases of pension benefits being lost, but I understand the noble and learned Lord the Lord Chancellor has indicated that that might be dealt with by insurance. At any rate, Clause 4 provides for this. It says that where grave financial hardship is likely to accrue as a result of a decree being granted, then the court is entitled to take the most drastic step of refusing a decree altogether. If I may say so, I hope that this will not be regarded by the courts in any sense as a formality. I hope that the courts will regard this as a real provision with teeth, and that they will refuse decrees in those circumstances. Where it is quite clear that some innocent party is to be deprived of a benefit, I hope that a judge will not be argued out of refusing to make a decree on those grounds. I think the financial provisions in this Bill are unarguably sound.

(Speech in the House of Lords, June 30, 1969)

8. Rhodesia – The Settlement Proposals

For many weary months, I have been labouring in extremely distasteful negotiations – distasteful for a number of reasons: not because they were hostile, not because they were unfriendly, but because they involved such a difference of approach of principle and of social morality between the two sides as to make it necessary to shelve all such considerations in our discussions and to restrict them wholly to the technical issues. I believe, and I shall commend to your Lordships, that this settlement, being the best we were able to achieve – and, I am vain enough to believe, the best that most people would have been likely to achieve; and the responsibility for this is not personal to me – it would be an act of consummate folly to reject it.

I do not feel triumphant or enthusiastic about the terms of the settlement. Although I lack anything like his dialectic and legal skill, I could have done a better job of criticizing these terms than was done by the noble and learned Lord, Lord Gardiner. But, if I may venture to say so, that operation is largely irrelevant, because the issue that must be decided is: what is the alternative? The noble and learned Lord posed that issue with remarkable clarity when he mentioned the case of the unfortunate Mr Nkomo. Quite rightly, as a man of heart and principle, the noble and learned Lord abominates — as I do, and as I am sure every Member of your Lordships' House does — the notion that a human being should be under restraint for seven years, without trial and in these circumstances. But, without unkindness to the noble and learned Lord, I will put a question to him. Over those seven years he was the highest legal officer in this great country. He had available to him the whole resources of this country. How could he have contrived to secure the release of Mr Nkomo during that period? And what single step to advance that release was he, with all his feelings in the matter, which I respect, able to achieve? The fact that we earnestly urge another régime to release a man, but fail to do so is of no benefit to that man. To reject these proposals because we have been unable to secure his release, in the knowledge that by rejecting them, we leave him still languishing in incarceration is a moral gesture that is a purely personal self-indulgence. I believe that a great deal of the opposition to these proposals consists of moral gestures that are purely personal self-indulgence.

One of the great comforts and consolations to those who are concerned in trying to achieve this result was the knowledge that at the end the matter would be submitted to the arbitrament of the people of Rhodesia, of all the people of Rhodesia. Much thought was given to the best way to do it. I believe that the best way to do it is the way selected: for a Commission of honourable and able men to go round the country inquiring, wherever they think it necessary, whether, on balance, the people of Rhodesia consider that these proposals are substantially better than the conditions now prevailing. That is the test that ought to be applied. But the other day I noticed that Her Majesty's Opposition contemplated sending an alternative team to make the same inquiries. If I were Her Majesty's Government, I should not discourage it. I believe that if these proposals are fairly explained to the people of Rhodesia, it is extremely unlikely that they will reject them.

On the question of the availability of political voices of all shades, I would refer the noble and learned Lord, Lord Gardiner, to the terms of the White Paper which make it quite clear that the

Commission would be enabled to decide for itself what ought to happen in these matters. The White Paper says on page 7:

> 'Before and during this test of acceptability normal political activities will be permitted to the satisfaction of the Commission ... '

If the Commission finds that it is unable to secure that all political views are ventilated and that the people in Rhodesia are unable to hear all political views, then I think, knowing the quality of the Commission that is likely to be appointed, it will not be very long before they return to say that they cannot fulfil their task. I shall be profoundly surprised if this matter presents difficulties.

Of course, we encountered problems where the people in detention were regarded as untouchable, as unspeakable villains by the persons with whom we were negotiating. The fact that they had political aspirations different from those of their Rhodesian masters was enough to stamp them as outside the pale of human intercourse. That we did not accept this, that we found these notions horrible, did not affect the fact that we were unable to make inroads on their way of thinking. It would be hypocrisy to say that we set out on a political mission to reform Mr Smith and his friends in their way of political thought. If we did so set out, I regret to inform your Lordships that we returned with a total lack of success. I do not think that we have persuaded Mr Smith to a more liberal way of thought. What we have persuaded Mr Smith and his friends to realise is that the world will no longer accept a régime that imposes a total and inhuman despotism by a quarter of a million people over something like five million others. This we have achieved. I believe that the results of our activities, if accepted in good faith, if we are prepared to take certain political risks, offer the only hope for the emancipation of Rhodesia from the certainty of horrible and violent insurrection.

The three questions, I think, by which this Agreement must be considered are these. First, should one do business with Mr Smith and his friends at all? I had no hesitation in arriving at a conclusion that it was simply pious moralising to say, No. Who else was there to do business with? If one looked around and took the view that the Rhodesian African must look for his manumitting from either his own internal resources or from

Africans outside Rhodesia, what are the realities? The present Rhodesian Government are able to marshal an army, staggeringly enough, of 70,000 men. That is the strength of the force that can be called to the colours in Rhodesia. Rhodesia has, at least, the second best air force in Southern Africa. It has the total loyalty of the black policemen and the black soldiers who are enlisted in it.

In those circumstances, forgetting how long majority rule will take, how long will it be before the African, unarmed, peaceful, friendly and in no mood for insurrection, is able to revolt and procure his personal liberty? This is the question that I would invite those who consider these terms inadequate to ponder very carefully. What are the possibilities of assistance from outside to relieve the Rhodesian African? There again, there are no possibilities on the Portuguese frontier and none on the South African frontier. There are none on the Zambian frontier. That country is in deep financial difficulty; divided within itself; its own Opposition no more humanely treated than Mr Smith treats his own political adversaries. Is it to be supposed that the Zambians are likely to rally forces to assist the Rhodesians?

If you believe I am wrong; if you think that the Rhodesian African could revolt tomorrow, and revolt successfully, I should be the last man to deter him. I may say that the notion of bloodshed and violence appalls me. I believe that if desperate men, for the first time in confrontation with a great political power, have arrived at a solution of a desperate matter by negotiation, by the use of words in preference to the use of arms; if we have been able to redeem Rhodesia from the spectacle of small black children and small white children shattered by bullets and bombs, I think that we shall have achieved something which may be memorable within this century. I believe that this is something on which we should certainly take the risk. That is the first point. The first question is: should we do business with Mr Smith? My answer is, previous governments have done so and it would, in my view, be wrong and mere self-indulgence if we did not.

The second question we have to ask is: if we do business with Mr Smith, are these terms appropriate on which to do it? Are they the best terms that we can get? Are they the best terms we can get if we wait or do it at some later stage? And if they are the best terms that we can get, are they good enough? To my first question I have already given an answer. I believe them to be the best terms that we can get. I do not think that waiting would make any appreciable difference. It is a difficult problem and it demands a very nice balance of assessment regarding sanctions. On the one side, for instance, there is breaching of sanctions by the American action; by the fact that the Zambians purchase corn and acquire their electricity from Rhodesia, and on the whole do not take sanctions as seriously as we do. There would seem to be any number of breaches of the sanction net if you go into Rhodesia and see the supplies there and the purchases they are making. That on the one side. On the other side, there is the possibility that if sanctions are working, nevertheless the Rhodesians will progress further and further into the South African sphere of influence. I would say that that danger is so much greater than the other danger, that that possibility is so much greater than the other possibility, that it is unwise to wait.

My Lords, you will remember that it is nearly eleven years since the 1961 Constitution, it is six years since UDI, and nothing at all has happened in this period except endless debate and endless negotiation. Hence we have to ask ourselves, if nothing better can now be achieved, is this good enough? I do not believe it is very good. I do not believe that we ought to go dancing a jig through the lobbies in support of these recommendations. But I believe that we should support them because they are good enough to give the African and the white Rhodesian (there are many white Rhodesians totally innocent of participation in this matter, totally innocent of a desire to dominate their African colleagues, to whom we should give the most careful consideration) the opportunity of majority rule overtaking massacre. That is my belief.

Now, my Lords, may I venture to make this observation? The noble and learned Lord, Lord Gardiner, drew attention with considerable force to the length of time that it was going to take for majority rule—as though nothing was going to happen until that time was achieved. May I give him a few more comforting facts. First, the political control of Rhodesia will, on the whole, be with the new African higher roll, but there will be enfranchised —although in a most limited sense, and voting for a few seats only—an additional 250,000 Africans who will immediately go on the lower B roll, and who, if they so desire, will attain what I regard as very important, the status of a voter and an understanding of the democratic process. If a man once goes to a poll and casts a vote he is much more likely to regard that as the ordinary routine of government than some other more violent and disagreeable matter.

Apart from that, there will be a progressive progress towards majority rule. I am told that at the moment there may be as many as 15,000 Africans eligible for immediate registration on the higher roll. That was a much more comforting figure than when we first entered into our negotiations. This will provide, at the rate of 3,000 per seat, immediately another six seats, if I am not mistaken, or something approaching six seats. Assume that it is only four seats. The position that then will prevail will be this. There are sixteen seats in the House already arising from the lower roll. With four more seats that is twenty seats. With the fact that in the solid majority of Europeans is included the Asian and the coloured, both of whom rank for all purposes in Rhodesia as Europeans and, thanks to this new Constitution, whatever views Mr Smith and his friends may have, will continue to rank as Europeans, there is already a significant minority which, if for a moment we can get away from thinking on the basis of monolithic, racial politics, is one which certainly would not be regarded as derisory within our own democratic institutions, and certainly one which it would be considered necessary to woo. That minority will be increased at the rate of 3,000 voters as time progresses.

The noble and learned Lord, Lord Gardiner, acquainted me with the predictions of the various wizards who have been undertaking statistical investigations in this matter. I would say only this to the noble and learned Lord. In the course of our many months of negotiation we had the benefit of the services of a number of statisticians of the most worthy character. I arrived at the conclusion very soon which, alas!, is slightly harsh upon these gentry, that their conclusions were totally valueless. It would seem to me an absolute absurdity for anyone who is not in direct alliance with the Almighty to predict with precision that majority rule is coming in sixty-four years. If I may venture to say so, the very precision of that estimate discredits it totally from the outset. I do not know how long it will be. It is my firm and fervent belief that it will be much less than sixty-four years. But I can comfort the noble and learned Lord by telling him that only the other day the Rhodesian Front were estimating it at ten years. I think that ten years is equally fanciful; but whatever the period is, if there is an uninterrupted progress to majority rule, if the African sees with certainty that the additional seats are added and the time limit is not one which makes him despair of ever seeing it within a reasonable rate of progress, is that so awful? I venture to think not.

I venture to think that it would be better if we could have contrived to get it in fifteen or sixteen years or whatever it is. It is not beyond possibility that this could still happen. The nature of the boom which may descend on Rhodesia, of changes in its prosperity and the treatment of its industry — all these may bring the most revolutionary and dramatic changes in the progress in relation to these registers. But I will say to the noble and learned Lord that it would be most unfortunate to send a message out from this House to the Africans of Rhodesia that they are condemned never to have majority rule; that the whole of this plan is totally deceptive and that on the whole they have nothing to hope for.

There is nothing in that proposal which prevents unimpeded progress towards majority rule. So far as the first proposal is concerned, if I may venture to say so, except on the rather factitious basis that it is not fast enough — and nobody really knows how fast it is — an honest effort has been made to give it reality and I would venture to say that it comes four-square within Sir Alec's First Principle.

I do not intend to spend a great length of time in dealing with the other questions of what comes within the Principles. The Second Principle, which I believe to be the one of retrogression, is wholly satisfied. In order to achieve that there is a retrogression in the Constitution it is necessary to ensure that there is a separate majority of both voting categories. This is of importance not only before but after majority rule. It then becomes of great importance to the Europeans to ensure that the Constitution cannot be altered to their disadvantage. Hence it requires a separate majority of Europeans as well as of Africans, but the majority of the Africans must be a genuine majority. The idea that you can write off as having no political significance, no allegiance and no loyalty to their race, the indirectly elected Africans would, I think, be rejected almost entirely by every citizen, whether black or white, except those who have manifest political interests for saying so.

As pointed out by the noble Earl in opening the debate, since the sixteen black Members of the House have sat they have voted solidly on every racial issue. They were quite indifferent, if I may say so, to the loss of their stipends. The other, slightly unfortunate, suggestion that these people are so corrupt that the suggestion that they would be deprived of public benefits would provoke them into a total betrayal of their race, has not been proved correct. That has not happened. They have not betrayed their race, whatever risks attach to their course of action. They have accepted those risks. I believe that this is a valid and effective blocking mechanism. It may well be that, in the end, some Africans will be persuaded to vote against their own interests. I would say that Africans should be urged to watch the situation with the greatest of care. Their lives and their futures, and their continued political prospects are in their own hands, but they have been given a fair chance.

In the long months in which I have been travelling to and from Rhodesia, achieving miracles of anonymity of disguise which some of you might have regarded as nearly impossible, I arrived at certain conclusions in this matter. I arrived at the conclusion that an agreement, respectable in the sense that it maintained a valid and honourable promise of the possibility of advance to majority rule, a respectable and honourable promise that there would be an honest look at racial discrimination and respectable and honest safeguards to ensure any possibility of retrogression, was an agreement that we should adopt with alacrity. When we set off on our negotiations I did not believe that we would achieve the agreement that in fact has been achieved. I do not believe it to be inadequate. I do not believe that there has been a sell-out. I do not believe that we had anything to sell. We certainly did not have the African, who is in bondage to the Rhodesians, to sell. But I believe there was a sell-out—not by this agreement or by this Government in negotiating the agreement, but in past years, which left us in the disagreeable position that we could negotiate no better agreement than this one. Over the years since 1921, and some people say back to the Jameson

Raid, when the future of Southern Rhodesia and other parts of Africa was so hopelessly compromised, it was open to us to deal with this situation.

We must not talk of the Land Tenure Act as though it were an innovation. It first came into operation in the 1920s and was renewed in 1941. It has been there under the auspices of successive Governments of every colour, including a Liberal Government. We must not consider it as one of the novelties introduced by Mr Smith. It is now embodied in the whole structure of Rhodesia. It would have been a near impossibility for us to deal with the Land Tenure Act in detail, unless we had stayed there for months and months and months. The only sensible thing to do was to set up an honourable Commission, including an African, and request them to look at it. If I may say so, one could read anything into the words which the noble and learned Lord, Lord Gardiner, invited the noble Earl to construe.

I think that no Government could have been expected, though we asked them, to accept in advance and *en bloc* the findings of a Commission which they had not seen and of whose findings they had no notion. I think they have inserted the minimum possible qualifications that skilful draftsmanship could devise. I believe that these proposals are the best that we can do. And if they are the best that we can do, we should seize with gratitude the opportunity of redeeming the shortcomings of our previous colonial activities in this territory, and hope for the future, not that people will act with dishonesty, not that people will act with breach of faith and breach of integrity, but that the white Rhodesians will realize also that this is the last opportunity to avoid disaster.

(Speech in the House of Lords, December 1, 1971)

PART TWO

The Institutions

1. *Reform of the House of Lords*

I do not believe that democratic institutions in this country are tottering to ruin; and that youth and student power and violent demonstrations will supplant them; but I do believe that it would be foolish and complacent not to recognize that a respect for Parliamentary democracy is crucial if the way of life that most of us believe in is to be preserved.

That respect is waning not because the institutions have failed but because they are being subjected to the strain that a reforming government must put on any legislative machinery. As a result, institutions and machines that should work slowly and deliberately to polish and improve complicated Bills are being pressed into a speed of action both unseemly and inappropriate. But it is ironical that the only proposal for reform should come where it is least relevant.

The constitutional struggle of 1910–11 drew the teeth of the House of Lords. It was probably the most ferocious, ill-mannered and exciting episode in British Parliamentary history. It left bitterness and corrosions that survive to this day, but it settled emphatically and finally that the full powers of government were to repose in an elected assembly, and that a right to inheritance could no longer include a right to rule.

The Parliament Act of 1911 was accepted by the Tory party only after the threat of desperate expedients, as in 1832 with the Reform Bill. The Prime Minister had to threaten the creation of a small army of peers to neutralize the Tory majority. Under this threat the Tories accepted a dwindling down of the Lords' legislative powers almost to vanishing point. It could have no say in money Bills; any other enactments it could delay for up to two years – and that was the whole of it.

What is relevant to recall is that the Parliament of the day had no intention of leaving matters with the definition of the law-making functions. The preamble to the Parliament Bill read:

Whereas it is intended to substitute for the House of Lords as it at present exists a second Chamber constituted on a popular instead of an hereditary basis, but such a substitution cannot immediately be brought into operation.

The last words have proved a total truth. Fifty-seven years have elapsed and although various resolutions have been passed, both in the Commons and in the Lords, declaratory of proposed changes, including a declaration by the Lords themselves as far back as March, 1910, that 'the possession of a peerage should no longer of itself give the right to sit and vote in the House of Lords', nothing effective has been done since the Parliament Act except the curtailment in 1947 of the delaying power to one year instead of the previous two.

One does not need to seek far for the explanation. Parliament does not ordinarily neglect for half a century its own firmly expressed intention in any matter which retains current significance. But this matter has not retained current significance. The delineation of the Lords' powers did almost all of the job. Provided that the Chamber which exercised the delaying powers was of moderate competence and responsibility, its constitution was of very little importance.

If the rules of statistics are blended into rules of genetics and applied to a body of hereditary peers, most of whom are well-educated and possess inherited lands and responsibility, it is a total certainty that a respectable proportion will be intelligent, reputable and responsible people capable of discharging public duties as well as, if not better than, other sections of the community. It is no less certain statistically that a number of them will possess the ordinary deficiencies and shortcomings, to the point of mania, to which some proportion of any designated selection of humanity must succumb.

The House of Lords was until recently operating on the basis of inheritance, but it was sifted inheritance, because the inept, the irresponsible, the criminal – a tiny number indeed – and the demented, in their genetic proportions, either did not come, or were advised not to come, or were positively excluded. Every so often, if a crucial division arose, a gathering of weird and eldritch figures filled the lobbies and ensured – as they do today at any time of ferocious Whipping – that the Tory party commands a satisfactory majority.

Apart from the hereditary peerages of first creation, a substantial number of nominated life peers are now members. All in all the House of Lords, exercising, since 1964 at least, powerful self-restraints, has performed a useful 'editorial' function without any attempt to assert undue sway or influence. It has with proper humility recognized that its existence and constitution are an historical accident, and that it represents nobody; but for a body representing nobody it does a great amount of virtually unpaid work, and does it with considerable skill, expedition and good humour. But reform of some kind is nevertheless desirable. Whether the discussions that have been going on for some while between the two parties will lead to any conclusion has been doubted. I hope they will. This seems to me a matter that should be determined by a compromise.

I am profoundly convinced that there is no virtue in seeking now to curtail the innocuous functions of the Lords and that there is virtue in retaining those functions in their present form and – dare one say it? – to some extent in enlarging them. If we accept that the Lords will continue as a Chamber with power in the ultimate analysis only to offer suggestions for the improvement of legislation, we must also accept that there is immense scope for this activity. It is anomalous that money Bills, the Bills most in need of the Lords' expertise and judgement, should not have the full benefit of them. Anyone who reads the horrors of syntax contained in any Finance Act should be grateful to a point of importunity for any help to make these meaningless labyrinths of language more intelligible. Moreover it is desirable that a well-informed body of public men, acquainted with the use and purpose of money, should at least furnish advice on legislation relating to it.

It is accepted on all sides that a plan to reform the Lords is unavoidable, since even the present mild functions become unfair and possibly intolerable if their full exercise constitutes a threat to one party only. There is no reason at all why, in relation to the Transport Bill or any other piece of legislation, the Lords should not exercise the powers given to them by Parliament until those powers are changed, but there appears to me, as there appears to the majority of my fellow peers, strong reason for ensuring that a built-in political majority should no longer survive in the House of Lords.

How best to achieve this result must be a matter of speculation and is certainly not a matter of urgency. It is ironical that the very people who express the most determined hostility to hereditary membership show a comparable distaste for elected membership when it applies to the Lords. Possessing as we do an unwritten constitution fortified by unwritten conventions, but one which has worked and worked successfully over the centuries, I can understand and sympathize with a disinclination to dig up the foundations. I am myself an unrepentant believer in a two-Chamber system of government – both Chambers being fully elected. I do not accept that either inheritance or nomination is a safe and secure way of appointing legislators. I am, if anything, more dubious about nomination than heredity. There are no statistical rules to blend with genetics where nomination is concerned.

At the moment all the criticism is levelled at the Commons and not the Lords. There is real disquiet about the volume of undigested legislation that passes through the Commons machine, and a great deal of grumbling about the strain placed on Members in seeking to discharge their duties conscientiously over too many statutes. One wonders whether – if the Lords reform proposals have not reached finality or are not near finality – it would not be wise to start again and to set up an important Royal Commission to consider the whole of the Parliamentary process.

I believe that many peers do not much mind what is done about the constitution of the House of Lords. Most of them would deplore its abrogation – and I think rightly. Most of them would deplore a reduction of its functions and I think – in terms of public welfare – rightly, but few of them have an exaggerated notion of the part it plays or can at present play, and many would like to see it integrated into a legislative machine of greater efficiency.

Mr Anthony Wedgwood Benn was certainly right to draw attention to an increasing belief that the legislative machine ought always to draw on the springs of its ultimate authority, and that this it sometimes does not do and more often seems not to do. The cure is not a referendum. It may be to consider whether our cherished notions of an unwritten constitution can in a complicated modern society be fully preserved.

(*Daily Telegraph*, June 18, 1968)

2. The Press

It is, I think, a disaster that no new newspaper can be launched today; but this is a truism not only in relation to newspapers. No new industry can be launched today. It is true to say that you cannot start a shoe factory. It is true to say that you cannot start a bicycle factory. I think there are factors germane to this discussion other than the mere fate of the Press. I do not want to dwell on them, but I profoundly agreed with the noble Lord, Lord Balfour of Inchrye, when he said that what we are discussing today is the symptom of a much wider malaise.

Another part of his speech with which I greatly agreed concerned his comments about the workpeople, which I thought were generous. I have been personally distressed by what I thought was over-stringent criticism of the workpeople in the newspaper industry. A legend has been put about that they are responsible for the misfortunes of the industry, that they have been blackmailing the industry and that they have been engaged in other enormities. There is no doubt that restrictive practices in trade unions are deplorable and have particularly affected the Press; but to suggest that the state in which the newspaper industry finds itself at this moment is due to the trade unions is, I think, both an over-simplification and a total unfairness to the unions as a whole.

I should like to state my belief that this is so, and that a too-often repetition of this sort of slander – because I think it is a slander – is not favourable or helpful to anyone. We want to discourage restrictive practices; and I think that, in consultation with the unions, as the newspaper proprietors are wisely engaged in, these practices can be relieved, can be altered and can be mitigated. But I do not think too much responsibility should be attributed to any particular quarter. If I may say so without disrespect to the noble Lord, Lord Thomson of Fleet, who made a most remarkable speech with the greatest integrity today, no newspaper compositor has contrived by any restrictive practices to become the proprietor of 140 newspapers. I think, if I may say so, that that is the most valid comment one can make on the accusations which have been levelled at them.

What we have to ask ourselves is this. Newspapers are disappearing and will disappear. I speak with the rather slender personal qualification of being the chairman of the trustees of a Sunday newspaper. This makes me no expert on newspapers, but fills me with a deep concern for the preservation of the existing newspapers. I do not think we can view with composure and satisfaction the prospect of newspapers disappearing. On the other side of the House the opinion has been expressed, principally by the noble Lord, Lord Thomson of Fleet, but also in other quarters, that it does not much matter. I think it does matter. It matters vitally in a free democracy. We do not want to make light of the word 'democracy'. It is something we cherish. It is something to which we should attach cardinal and vital importance. And it is our duty to take special pains to preserve those attributes to a free democracy which are necessary to its preservation.

However appalling the risks may be (to use the Prime Minister's own expression), I do not think that State intervention in the world of newspapers will bring about an interference with their freedom or liberty. Those risks are only half the danger of allowing newspapers to disappear or to become consolidated in a few hands only. If I had to choose between the risks of State intervention and State subsidy or the risks of the indiscriminate disappearance of newspapers, as has been happening and is happening, then I would opt for State interference. But I do not believe that State interference is or will necessarily become a necessity. If newspapers will set their own houses in order, it is possible that they will prevent this disagreeable occurrence – because disagreeable it must be. But to set their own houses in order they will have to take a far more realistic viewpoint than we have heard expressed in this House today.

First, they will have to recognize what is happening. We have heard loose phraseology. To use the phrase of the noble Lord, Lord Balfour of Inchrye, there has been a lot of cant about saving *The Times*. But *The Times* has not been saved. *The Times* is a small, specialized publication having a circulation, I believe, of 300,000 odd, or something of that sort. That is not the newspaper which Lord Thomson of Fleet is saving, or the newspaper he is set on preserving. He is set on establishing a large, multi-circulation newspaper which will declare war on the *Daily Telegraph*. Are we to believe that this situation is to be saved by starting a war between the new, Thomson-owned *Times* and the *Daily Telegraph*? What can happen as a result of that war? One or other must go to the wall. The noble Lord, Lord Thomson of Fleet, says that *The Times* is safe. *The Times* is apparently safe only by creating risks for another newspaper.

I think that the valuable message that can be sent out from this House is not that of horror and terror at the possibility of State intervention, not that of fear that we are going to interfere with some notional independence – for, after all, the word 'independence' has a strange meaning where you relate it to an acceptance of one man owning 140 newspapers and a positive phobia and paralysis at the suggestion that the State might make a small subsidy to one or two others. It is a word with a very specialized meaning in that context. I would say that the message we have to send out today is that there must be a measure of agreement among the newspaper proprietors and in the newspaper world that they themselves want these newspapers to survive and will take reasonable and civilized steps, by arrangement between themselves, to see that they do. Otherwise, I would urge the Government to have ready plans to deal with the matter.

I should like to say a word on the question of subsidy, because I think that a great deal of misunderstanding has been expressed on this subject, particularly by the noble Viscount, Lord Rothermere. The noble Viscount, Lord Rothermere, said that if a subsidy was given to a variety of newspapers they would all lose their independence. This is a startling doctrine in this country at this time. We have subsidized a number of most important institutions, many of them concerned with the mind. The graphic instance that comes to mind is, of course, our universities. Our universities are State subsidized. Is there a person here who would suggest that our universities are not independent, that they are subservient to the people who provide the money, that they enjoy less freedom of expression or that they are fearful of speaking their minds because they get grants from the State? This would be arrant nonsense. I speak as the chairman of an organization which lives by giving away subsidies; and, if I may say so, there never was a collection of customers who were so ready, and happily so, to bite the hand that feeds them as those of the Arts Council. I have yet to find a single instance of a customer of the Arts Council who would defer to the Arts Council or the Government because he had had a grant from us – and I shall be very sorry if the day ever arrives when there is such an occurrence.

I would suggest that we are able, in our wisdom, to find means of bestowing money upon newspapers from non-political circles and through a non-political organization which leaves those newspapers in the hands of independent-minded people who are in no way dependent upon or subservient to the people who give money to them. To suggest otherwise is a reflection on the spirit and character of the people. I make this statement as a profound statement of my own beliefs in this matter. That is not to say that I would not recognize the appalling risks. I think, for instance, that it would be quite wrong to have a government-owned printing press so that at any stage printing facilities might be withdrawn. I cannot see why, if it is a question of deciding whether newspapers are to continue to exist or to fall by the wayside according to the operation of the so-called economic laws, it should not be possible, on a perfectly respectable basis, to devise a means of giving them some kind of subsidy. If such a step became necessary, it would have my support; because I regard the alternative as a source of far greater injury and danger to the democratic society in which I wish to live.

I think we have a good Press; and I think that, over the years, we have a representative Press. In my view it is catastrophic that we cannot today even contemplate the possibility of establishing a new newspaper. I hope that we shall not send out from this House in any form a message that 'all is for the best in the best of all possible worlds'; that we have only to sit back and the newspapers will recover from a temporary slump, and that everything will be well again. I do not believe this to be the case. But I think that a situation can be achieved where, by sensible agreement among the people concerned – the industry, the workers: all elements – it may be possible and should be possible to put the industry back on its feet. But it behoves a constant watchfulness, and it behoves a readiness on the part of those like ourselves who may have decisions to make to be prepared to take risks.

(Speech in the House of Lords, January 25, 1967)

3. Law Reform

I believe that any conscientious practitioner of the law of England will have some ideas for its reform; but this is no special reflection on English Law, a system of special grandeur and magnificence which has become part of the intellectual heritage of the Western World, and a powerful influence on the shape of many non-Western societies. It is simply that if the law is not to be a machine of tyrannical rigidity but instead is to be the useful and malleable servant of a changing social scheme it must from time to time be adapted and the periods between radical adaptions cannot be too protracted. But a special responsibility attaches to anyone who advocates changes in the law. Let me therefore emphasize that although I think the English legal system at this moment of time needs change in a number of ways, it is a system which continues to deserve proper confidence in all important particulars, and I know of no responsible person minded towards law reforms who would dissent from this basic proposition.

Bearing this in mind, let me say, first, that I do feel that it is no longer appropriate, and indeed faintly ridiculous, that grown members of a learned profession should wear period costumes. This is particularly so since they adopt the convention of our undergraduate days, that the honourable nature of a garment is reflected by its age and tatters. But I also believe that there is a more important aspect of the wig and gown than the question of maintaining a tradition or discarding it. I think it reflects an attitude on the part of the people who wear it which is no longer a relevant or contemporary one. It serves to maintain differences and distinctions which I believe should be minimized and not stressed.

But there are, of course, arguments to the contrary, although the valid ones are not necessarily those which are principally advanced. I was puzzled, for instance, by a defence of wig and gown raised in *The Times*, by an ex-law officer of very great learning and distinction, that the object of the wig and gown as worn by the judge was to maintain anonymity. Whether it is good or bad to maintain anonymity on the part of a judge is an arguable question. But English judges – who are men of exceptional quality – have appearances and personalities so individual that decking them out in this type of costume is a most futile expedient for disguising their individual characteristics. I doubt whether the costume of Ku-Klux-Klan would achieve this objective, but in any event anonymity is not a characteristic of the English judicial approach. It is a characteristic of continental legal systems where the judges – less colourful and less individual characters, give their judgment in the name of the Court and subordinate the views and opinions of the individual judge to a composite conclusion.

In England the stress is entirely the other way. The personality and identity of the judge features very largely in the matter. The judgment is given in his own name. It is shot through and through with personal pronouns and personal opinions. A good judgment is instinct with a philosophy and inbred beliefs of a strong individual mind. And judgments are assessed according to their authors. Although a fiction to the contrary may operate that the judgments of a Court of a particular jurisdiction enjoy equal authority – in fact, in the course of argument in the Court of Appeal or the House of Lords special reference is frequently made to the identity of the particular judge and a special importance attached to judgments given by judges of accepted reputation and standing in particular fields of law. Nothing could be less consistent with a claim for judicial anonymity.

But the question of raiments, while interesting and even entertaining, deserves no great prominence in the discussion of law reform. The question of the reorganization of the profession deserves great prominence. The reorganization of the English profession cannot be fairly assessed without recognizing the immense virtues that it possesses in its present shape. First, we have a judiciary of great wisdom; great fairness of mind and absolute probity. It is to be doubted – and this is not a narrow chauvinistic claim – whether any country in the world possesses better judges viewed over the whole range of our judicial system. The American Supreme Court has judges of whom it would be difficult to find individual counterparts, but having had some view of the operation of other American courts I do not think that Americans could or would claim that their judiciary, on the whole, is on a par with our own. Otherwise the system of the appointment of judges of most other European territories and in many other parts of the world differs so fundamentally from our own that comparisons are difficult. One can arrive at a reasonably safe conclusion that the method of appointment by special training for judicial service as distinct from selection from a small *élite* of practitioners weighs the scales enormously in favour of our own Bench.

Then, so far as the practising professions are concerned, we have a Bar with an undeviating sense of dedicated purpose and the most gratifying sense of values in placing the importance of the administration of justice way out in front of any question of personal rewards (an attribute which it is pleasing to record is shared by my own profession). It has also a sense of duty to the Court which transcends its obligation to any individual client. Added to this is a camaraderie within the profession which for its members, and even to an objective viewer, is a highly attractive characteristic, but about which it is possible to feel that it creates an 'inbreeding' in the law which is not wholly beneficial to the society it serves. This Bar is small in number, highly qualified so far as its active practitioners are concerned, and immensely influential to a point of near dominance over the whole shape of legal institutions. It is largely within the Bar that powerful resistance to the changes which I suggest at least need to be considered, has been and will be increasingly forthcoming – and not for discreditable reasons. The Bar genuinely believes that it is *corps d'élite*, necessary for the preservation of the virtues that I have unstintingly acknowledged are possessed by the judiciary and by its members, and which emerge day after day in the conduct of judicial proceedings.

But the Bar is fanatical in maintaining this view, and I have never been able to conduct a discussion with a member of the Bar (either before or after elevation to the Bench) where emotional arguments do not outnumber and outweigh any others. A very good illustration of this is the recent short-lived controversy about extending the jurisdiction of the County Courts so that they could hear undefended divorce cases. On the face of it this was a mild and innocuous and sensible reform. But it involved one proposition which was totally unacceptable to the Bar, that a new area of advocacy would be made available to solicitors (who of course have a right of audience in County Courts, but not in the divorce courts as at present constituted).

It was amusing to see how protagonists against the change honestly failed to recognize that this was the real reason of their opposition, and a miscellany of comic arguments were put forward to replace the one valid one. Without this change, undefended divorce cases are, in fact, largely heard by County Court judges – enjoying the status of High Court Commissioners in order to ensure that solicitors do not appear before them – and conducting their divorce proceedings often in cramped and improvised huts and buildings erected specially in the courtyards of the Law Courts. The only dignity was contributed by the unvarying cool judicial approach of the judge and the legal practitioners. Nevertheless, a clamour was set up that by removing these proceedings to the self-same judges' own more spacious and custombuilt County Courts – which despite their architectural shortcomings appeared as temples of the law beside the huts in the Strand – it would deprive the proceedings of dignity and would lower the status of marriage. It is, of course, difficult to treat such arguments seriously. In fact, one is happy to think that they will be of no avail, and a sensible little reform will be brought into being which will enable the petitioner to have the case heard in his or her local County Court, possibly save the witnesses a protracted journey, and to some extent reduce the cost of the operation. But, alas, against the opposition of the great majority of the Bar.

I have instanced this particular point at some length because it is very significant of an attitude instinctively adopted towards any question of amalgamating the two professions, or even changing the present structure of the individual professions. I do not wish to create the impression that these changes are wholeheartedly approved by solicitors, since this is not the case. I should think that if a Gallup Poll were taken of all solicitors, there would probably (but not certainly) be a majority in favour of maintaining the separate professions as they are, or in any event unamalgamated, but I cannot be sure and I have certainly perceived a recent attitude among my own colleagues more sympathetic towards a merger.

It may be thought strange that, in view of the opinion that I hold about the present merits of the judiciary and of the two legal professions – since the solicitors' profession is one of no lesser integrity, or dedication, though not of the same high degree of learning as the much smaller practising Bar – that I nevertheless unhesitatingly advocate the fusion of the two professions. I do so in the firm belief that the public interest would be served by this change, and that there are powerful and compelling reasons which would justify accepting the risk that the new profession and the new judiciary might not immediately attain the high quality of their predecessors. On balance it is my opinion that the advantages to be gained to the public and to the profession itself from the changes would be substantial, and in one respect are indispensable.

There are two overwhelming reasons why – despite all other considerations – a drastic change in the organization of the profession is inevitably in the public interest. The first is that all legal practitioners are deeply concerned about the cost of litigation to the non-aided litigant, to the point where many of us believe that it is nearly impossible to advise a client of moderate means to become engaged in certain types of litigation – however important it may be in the interests of that person to do so. Although there is much resistance to this view, the prohibitive costs of litigation on many legal fronts is due, if not predominantly then at least in part, to the absence of a fused profession. Since I hold this belief very strongly, I should make it clear that it is opposed with equal vehemence by many lawyers, who do not agree with it and do not think any effective economies would be achieved by fusion. It is for that reason that I think an issue of this kind should be subjected to an Inquiry by a Royal Commission.

Unarguably, the actual cost of litigation is terrifying. Extreme examples are sometimes unfair, but quite recently a case ended in this country, involving the by no means unusual or special problem of ascertaining the validity of a will, where the costs were estimated at £½ million. This is no doubt an exaggerated estimate, but the lawyers concerned were all of the highest repute in terms of competence and efficiency, and one can be sure that no money was wasted so far as the conventions of legal procedure prevented it. Yet, even if the costs were only half this amount, it points with certainty to a need for change and, whilst this is a sensational example, it is possible to show less sensational but equally alarming examples by the dozen. Only the other day a judge was declaiming about the cost of a libel action which had occupied several days and where the plaintiff found himself facing a bill for many thousands of pounds. But it is not only in these spheres – where it may be thought the litigant has some element of choice – but in such matters as domestic litigation – where often no possibility of choice exists – that ruin confronts a litigant of modest means who is unavoidably involved in matrimonial proceedings. A defended divorce case must cost many hundreds, and more frequently thousands, of pounds, and yet one or both parties may have no option about proceeding with it or defending it.

It is a sad fact that many litigants can only contemplate resort to law with terror; and that to many others – however vital the need – the doors of the courts are firmly closed by the weight of gold. This is of itself enough to render the matter one of social urgency, but to justify an investigation a prima facie case must be established that economies can reasonably be expected from fusion.

At the moment any place of High Court litigation involves retaining the services of a solicitor throughout the proceedings, and at least one counsel to settle documents, advise at all interlocutory stages, and conduct the advocacy in the first court and, if necessary, during the subsequent appeals. The advocate is instructed separately by the solicitor, paid separately, and is in no way professionally linked with the solicitor. But this is by no means the end of it, for in many cases where issues of difficulty or special importance are involved it is not possible to retain one single junior counsel. Because of these issues, or possibly even only because the adversary has retained the services of a leading counsel, two members of the Bar will appear together to conduct the proceedings. As a general rule, the junior member will expect to receive two-thirds the fee of his leader, so that in a great many cases three lawyers will be engaged. It can be said with some justice that the three men are engaged to do the work of one. It seems to me at least worthy of consideration that, if one only is employed, the fees concerned will, if not reduce by two-thirds, at least be substantially less than the aggregate at present charged.

I do not wish to overstate the case, and opponents of my viewpoint will argue that if you had a fused profession with advocates incorporated into various firms of solicitors, there would be a shortage of advocates, so that a great many solicitors would still need to employ an outside man, although now in status as a solicitor, to conduct their advocacy. It is my own belief that a heavy price is paid for the very expertise of the advocates, and that we could afford to accept a less highly skilled technique of advocacy, which increasingly would be practised by many more solicitors as they gain confidence, and with it the conviction that rather too much fuss had previously been made about the difficulties of the matter.

This is not to say that there is not at present a very high standard of High Court advocacy, but if the choice is between retaining plu-perfection in forensic encounters or reducing the cost of litigation to sensible proportions, I believe that the volume of opinion would be in favour of relaxing standards. This is a major matter that, after many years of practice, spurs me to campaign for a professional change which would not be as far-reaching or difficult or painful as many of us make it out to be. It is my belief that when we have put this change into effect we shall be puzzled about why we did not do it many many years earlier.

There are an immense number of other considerations which shoot backwards and forwards like tennis balls on this topic. It affects, of course, the means of livelihood of lawyers, their training, their apprenticeships and many other cognate considerations. There are only a few upon which I can touch here.

The first of them is the other major matter which makes me think that this change should be brought about. On account of the separation of the professions the entire judiciary, including County Court judges, the great majority of Police Court Magistrates, even many of the Masters of the High Court, Recorders, and other legal officers, are eligible for their posts only if they are practising barristers. But this involves perhaps something in the region of 250 appointments, to be filled out of a Bar which is estimated to be of some 2,000 practising barristers. And this 2,000 represents barristers of all ages, all capacities, and all stages of professional attainment. It could reasonably be argued that at any given time the total pool of barristers available to fill the appointments is less than the number of appointments available.

But it hardly needs further demonstration that maintaining a strong and virile judicial stream must become a near impossibility from this limited pool. Moreover, although the judiciary has rightly received the praise for the qualities I have referred to, it is very much open to question whether its method of training, its immurement within the walls of its own small Inns of Court, and its almost monastic organization, are invariably right for the needs of a modern society.

Increasingly, solicitors find that large areas of new legal work are outside the scope and knowledge of the Bar, so that the availability of specialized knowledge – one of the great arguments in favour of maintaining a separate Bar – may often no longer operate. Also, the organization of the profession as a whole has had the unfortunate result of depriving the public of the non-legal services of distinguished lawyers. Since barristers cannot take partners and for practical purposes cannot employ assistants or associates, the Bar is the most hard-working and most relentless of all professions. A fully employed barrister has time for almost nothing else, although a number do contrive to combine their duties with membership of the House of Commons – something which I believe becomes increasingly more difficult as time goes on. Certain it is that the contribution trained legal minds can make in many spheres of social activity is largely denied to the Bar. It is not without significance that solicitors today are occupying the prominent non-legal positions which were occupied by barristers. Probably the most distinguished practising lawyer in the rendering of public services is Lord Tangley, a practising solicitor – who sits as an Independent in the House of Lords. Only recently Lord Silkin, a practising solicitor, led the Socialist opposition in the House of Lords. Sir Alec Fletcher, before taking over law reform in the Government, discharged important public duties as well as conducting a busy practice. I myself contrive to combine my public duties at the Arts Council and elsewhere with an active practice because of the organizational possibilities available to solicitors and denied to barristers. This is a serious matter and one to which the Bar should give thought.

There are, of course, many barristers who have retired from practice, and some still practising, who do perform immensely important public duties, but I do know that my views on this matter and anxieties on this score are shared by many members of the Bar and many members of the Bench. This article will have served some purpose if it gives cause for thought among lawyers in general and also with the general public whom we exist to serve. It would be an injustice to lawyers as a whole to regard the need for change as a reflection on them. The cost of litigation is, unhappily, not caused for the enrichment of lawyers. There are few professions where the financial recompense is more worthily or deservedly earned. The general average of income, in my opinion, is moderate and should be higher. No lawyers contrive to make any capital fortunes unless they leave the profession or engage in activities outside the scope of the profession.

Ironically, the Bar would be infinitely better off if it adopted notions for fusion. Almost the only substantial financial inducement to remain a practising barrister is the tax concession enabling him to receive outstanding fees after retirement as tax-free capital. The removal of this concession would, in my opinion, be a disaster to the Bar and, as things stand today, unfair to them. A barrister can work for years with virtually no opportunity of saving anything. This single chance that is left to him is bare justice set against the opportunities of other people in other professions which do not deploy qualifications remotely comparable to those of a barrister. But the fact remains that all this dedication, all this hard work, and all this self-sacrifice ironically adds up to a result beneficial neither to the Bar nor to the public.

(*Sunday Times*, June 12, 1966)

4. Administration of Justice

Very often the delays in the conduct of litigation are attributed to the courts. Most practising lawyers know that only a very small part of these delays are the responsibility of the courts: they are often the responsibility of the practitioners concerned, and very often the responsibility of the parties. Lawyers and the courts earn undeserved opprobrium frequently because long delays are brought to notice which have nothing to do with the administration of the courts. That is something that can be said only by practising lawyers acquainted with the facts.

What I wish to say touches on matters about which the noble and learned Lord said nothing at all, because they are in a sense background matters. I am sure we need extra judges; I would not quarrel with that. I am sure that nobody is better able to judge that than the Lord Chancellor himself, and it would be an impertinence for anyone to presume to try to assess the number of judges which is required at any given time or not to accept from him without dissent what the requirements are.

The matter which concerns me is quite different; that is, the question of the appointment of judges. I do not apologize in the least for raising this matter. We very rarely have an opportunity of discussing this matter in public, and it is only when a Bill of this kind comes to Parliament, either in another place or before your Lordships' House, that one has the opportunity to review matters which I believe to be of cardinal importance to the whole of society. In determining how we appoint our judges, where they are appointed and who is eligible, I think it would be of great importance to ask whether procedures which have become hallowed by time and sacrosanct only by practice – not, if I may say so, by logical or scientific examination – do not need to be considered and studied in rather greater detail than we have had the opportunity of doing.

I have been moved to speak in this debate today by a memorandum I have received from the Law Society, which, as your Lordships know, is a body which administers the affairs of solicitors, of whom there are some 20,000. The Law Society is, from my knowledge – although I have never been concerned as anything more than a member; I have had nothing to do with the administration of its affairs at any time – a body which enjoys the respect of all its members, and which is regarded as extremely moderate and in the best sense very conservative, which maintains and which always has maintained an extremely sensible relationship between the two branches of the profession. I am perhaps known to have views that did not entirely accord with those of the Law Society. I was therefore agreeably surprised to discover that at long last the Law Society had decided that something ought to be done about the appointment of judges. It was an anomaly, perhaps an anomaly doing injustice to society as a whole, that every judgeship of every kind should be an appointment from the small body of barristers.

One of their major arguments is that the pool of barristers is a very tiny one. I believe it is a profession of which there are fewer than 2,000 practising members – I think that is a fairly accurate assessment, if not an over-assessment of the number practising. If your Lordships look at the Bill, you will see that it provides for, and there are in existence, something like 200 judicial appointments of judges; judges in your Lordships' House, in the Court of Appeal, Puisne judges, and County Court judges. But there are a great many other appointments that can be filled, or by convention are filled, only from members of the Bar. Magistracies are nearly always filled from members of the Bar. Queen's Bench masters are nearly always appointed from members of the Bar, if not exclusively. Recorders, some of whom are full-time and many of whom have onerous duties occupying a great deal of their time, are nearly always, if not exclusively, members of the Bar.

I calculated on one occasion, and said, that if one took into account those members of the barristers' profession who, in terms of age, mental capacity and other qualifications, were eligible to be appointed as judges, there were more judicial appointments to be filled than the whole number of practising barristers. This is an extremely serious matter. It is obviously a matter that requires careful review. That the pool of persons eligible to be appointed should be less than the number of appointments that exist for them is clearly something about which society must be most concerned.

It is my intention to put down an Amendment at an appropriate stage which will seek to persuade your Lordships' House that County Court judges, at least, should be appointed from among solicitors. But this is not because I am in the slightest degree concerned to advance the cause of solicitors; on the whole, I do not think they are doing particularly badly, or are in need of any poor relief, or require to be appointed as judges because of extraneous reasons. But I think it is the case that a profession that has provided at least one Prime Minister to this country, I believe one or two Chancellors of the Exchequer, and several Home Secretaries, can hardly be regarded as disqualified from appointing some county court judges if made the matter of specialist and careful selection.

The education of solicitors is at least on a par with barristers. On the whole, the standard of the solicitors' final examination, in regard to which I was for some years an examiner, is at least as high as, if not higher than, the requirement of the barristers' examination, for a rather specialist reason: that the Bar takes the view that when a man has passed his final professional examination he is not then by any means fully qualified, and the procedure of chamber instruction takes a much larger part in his education at that stage than it takes in the case of a solicitor, who receives his training in articles before taking his final examination.

For that reason, therefore, one can accept, and I hope the House will accept, that solicitors are, in terms of education, fully qualified for appointment at least as County Court judges. It is my belief that many will be eligible for High Court judgeships, and even higher appointments. But I think one should make modest starts, and I believe that when one starts from a position that there is a totally inadequate pool of persons from whom the appointments can be made, it is reasonable to suggest that some of those appointments, the minor and lesser of those appointments, should experimentally be held by solicitors. I do not think we should be incurring any risk to the quality of justice in this country; indeed, I believe that we should enhance it. I believe that there are considerable advantages in giving some judges a different approach and a different viewpoint, drawing them from different sectors of society, giving them knowledge of activities and so forth that they do not at present have because of the necessarily cloistered and secluded character of a barrister's training, would be a considerable advantage.

Many years ago, one eminent Lord of Appeal said of a brother judge that the less of sociology that any judge knew the better. While that may have been a relevant statement in those days, I believe it to be totally irrelevant today. It is most necessary that judges should know something of sociology, and it is at least necessary that they should know enough of sociology to assess the length of time that a case is taking and the ruinous consequences to the parties concerned in it in terms of the expense involved. I think we are moving in a direction where, on the whole, the liberalization of the profession in that regard is to be welcomed.

I am anxious to say what I have to say in non-controversial terms. I do not think it is for the benefit of the profession that there should be an issue on this matter. Particularly I do not want it to be suggested that I believe that there is anything wrong with the quality of our judges at the moment. I believe, and I am proud to say, having travelled widely and seen courts in many parts of the world, that there are few countries, if any, which can find judges of the quality, of the learning and the integrity that we are happy to possess. I think we should be very slow indeed to take any measures that would damage that position, very slow indeed to take any measures that might damage the quality and integrity of the holders of judicial office. I should not be making this suggestion if I felt that this was in the remotest degree a likely possibility. I do not think it is. As a small and minor measure, it will not set the houses of this town aflame, nor set anyone by the ears; and in the end we shall decide that it is something that ought to have been done long ago. Solicitors will, at least as a first step, be made eligible for appointments in the County Court bench, which I think would be a social advance.

I think the major argument is that most of the advocacy conducted in the County Courts is conducted by solicitors. It is therefore ironical and an anomaly that persons who are able to conduct cases, who are regarded as qualified to conduct the cases, should be debarred from being appointed to the Bench to adjudicate on them. It may well be that I am pushing at an open door, and that when these issues are taken into consideration and when the representations that will be made by the Law Society and are being made on all sides of the profession, are taken into account, this is a minor change that will be accepted gratefully. I do not think I need say any more about that.

There is one other thing that I should like to touch on. It is perhaps of a slightly more delicate nature; but I do not see why we should be timid about delicacies that affect everybody. It concerns the question of how judges come to be appointed at all. This is a subject shrouded in abysmal mystery. We do, of course, know that they are appointed by the noble and learned Lord the Lord Chancellor, whoever he may be at any given moment. But how he appoints them, and on what advice he appoints them, whether he has a committee of experts to guide him, how he makes himself acquainted with the competing claims of practitioners then current, he himself having necessarily withdrawn from the hurly-burly of court activity, is a matter on which I think it would be a good thing that something should be known.

I do not believe that in these days mysteries are a sound or a wholesome thing in these matters. In the years that I have been practising law I have (and I regret to have to say it), observed a number of highly deserving practitioners of the law – I am speaking of senior barristers – who in my opinion ought to have been judges. I do not know why they were not made judges. On many occasions where there are particularly strong candidates one hears strange rumours about how they failed to conform with some particular requirement or another. If a man has laboured all his life in a particular profession, if he appears ostensibly to have all the trends which are required for preferment, if he has done nothing wrong, if he has never committed any crime or any infraction of a professional code, it seems to me absolutely wrong that he should not in fact be appointed without some reason being assigned. It seems to me that there should be a good deal more publicity about these matters.

I am sure, for instance, that solicitors ought at least to be asked their opinion about the eligibility of candidates for this preferment. I am sure also that laymen ought to be asked. It seems to me odd, to put it no higher, that in matters that vitally affect all the laymen in this country these crucial appointments should be made, apparently, without reference to a single layman as to the eligibility of the candidate. We know the method that is adopted in the United States; we know that in fact appointments are there made by lay people, on the advice of lawyers. Whether this is the best way to do it, or whether it is better that lawyers should do it on the advice of laymen, I would not presume to say. But it seems to me totally wrong that these appointments should be made entirely on the recommendation of lawyers, enshrouded in secrecy and without anyone really knowing the circumstances in which this sort of thing happens.

I am not suggesting any scandals. I am not suggesting that the appointments that are made are not good appointments. I am only suggesting that at this moment of time, when we have long come to concede that privilege is something that people do not readily accept, and when institutions that have existed for years are no longer accepted at their face value and simply because of their antiquity, it is right that we should have a good hard look at this matter.

I should like to make one final observation. Having regard to the tiny pool of persons eligible for appointment to the Bench, it seems to me odd that we have never had an academic appointment to any level of Bench anywhere. We have some of the greatest and best academic lawyers in the world. The literature of English law is renowned as the finest published anywhere. We have great and learned lawyers operating in our universities who are entirely capable of discharging at least appelate functions, if not functions in courts of first instance. Yet we have never had an academic lawyer on the Bench, and yet they would be technically eligible since they are nearly always barristers. This is something to which I should like to draw the attention of the House and on which I would invite comment from the noble and learned Lord Chancellor.

When reading *Lives of the Lord Chancellors* some while ago, I found that there was an occasion when we got near to the appointment of an academic lawyer – I think it was some time in the 1920s – but the Bar ultimately drew back in horror and some very strange and tortured reasons were found for not appointing him. This is something which requires review. If one considers the wealth of wisdom which has accrued to the Supreme Court of the United States from lawyers like Mr Justice Frankfurter and other men of great academic distinction, who came from academic backgrounds, it seems odd that we should not make some use of the kind of talent which we possess in this country. I do not apologize to the House for having raised matters which may not strictly be within the terms of the Bill, but this is the first opportunity of saying something on matters which I feel are important and worthy of consideration.

(Speech in the House of Lords, January 29, 1968)

5. *Solicitors' Spirit of Indignation*

Solicitors – in spite of some human frailties – are a pacific body of men who have accepted with tolerance and good humour the pretensions of their peacock brethren at the Bar, but there is a new mood with the advent of new and younger solicitors. They are now questioning loudly whether it is justice to them and justice to the public that every judicial appointment should be filled and every piece of worthwhile advocacy discharged by a barrister. Moreover, there is for the first time a spirit of genuine indignation; and it has been largely promoted by the extraordinary and desperate arguments that have been deployed to justify the indefensible.

It would be a pity if the Courts Bill – which is receiving its second reading today – were to exacerbate the situation. The two professions have always lived in relative harmony, and it is imperative for the proper discharge of their duties that they should continue to do so, but there can be little doubt that if the Courts Bill is encouraged in its present form – ignoring the friendly noises made by the Beeching Commission in favour of the appointment of solicitors as circuit judges – the new equivalent of County Court judges – there will be real resentments, and a feeling that the position into which the Bar has manœuvred itself in exercising an almost monopoly influence on governmental decisions relating to the legal profession should no longer be acceptable. The Law Society itself, a body which does not press reform without careful and cautious consideration, has in this instant promoted the tabling of an amendment to the Bill.

No claim has been made for High Court appointments, but, when asked why he took the view that solicitors should not receive appointments to the County Court bench, the present Lord Chancellor – a man of wit and wisdom and a champion of liberty in many spheres – produced two objections. The first was that solicitors of suitable quality would be so prosperous that they would not want these appointments. It is difficult to see what harm would in any event be done by rendering them eligible but the argument exaggerates the prosperity of solicitors and does a wounding injustice to their public spirit.

Many solicitors render unpaid public services in positions of great distinction, and it is fanciful to believe that they would not – like their colleagues at the Bar – accept some sacrifice of income in return both for the prestige of the judiciary appointment and the opportunity to serve the community. The second argument was even weirder. The Lord Chancellor declared that if there were to be added to the available pool of barristers likely recruits from the solicitors' profession, the choice would be too large for him to know and select from on an informed basis. It is kinder not to deal with this argument and the amiable character of the Lord Chancellor provokes kindness.

The Bar is not remotely a *corps d'élite* – as is impliedly and often expressly claimed. It is a profession that recruits anyone who can find the fees to join an Inn of Court, has the gastronomic determination to eat the dinners, can pass an examination which by other professional standards is of relative simplicity, and can find a senior junior barrister with whom to serve the pupillage. It has recruited over the years and continues to recruit men of exceptional talent.

No solicitors would deny that the best of the legal fraternity are barristers, but inevitably with the tiny size of the profession these are relatively few in number. Its claims to great skill in advocacy certainly have no general application. There are many talented advocates but a great many of the humdrum variety who rely on learning and experience to compensate for eloquence.

In terms of the judicial catchment area there must be deducted the substantial number who are without the necessary intellectual and personal qualities; those who are too young and those who are too old, those who would not want to live in the locality in which an appointment arises and, in increasing numbers today, those who forsake the Bar after a successful career for newer and richer pastures. Apart from the defection of a distinguished High Court judge, there have been many instances of leading counsel of outstanding talent who – for one reason or another – have found employment in merchant banking and in great industrial companies.

Moreover, for High Court appointments the choice is almost invariably restricted to silks. And the Bar, in spite of its tiny size, is a profession of high specialization. Large numbers would not be qualified in the general legal activities which are required from most members of the judiciary.

It does not require a senior wrangler to calculate the pathetic inadequacy of the barristerial force from whom choice has to be made, bearing in mind that there are something like 400 judicial appointments of one kind or another and hundreds more if one includes deputies and temporary appointments for which barristers alone are legally eligible or actually appointed.

It is perfectly clear the number of appointments greatly exceed the possible candidates at any one time, and that if by some unthinkable catastrophe a holocaust took place in the judiciary it could not be refilled. But such a disaster is not the serious problem. It is that quite plainly there is far too limited a choice for judicial appointment, and that a young man of reasonable ability registering entry at the Bar today is engaged almost in a process of self-selection for some sort of judgeship. One might think that with the availability of a large labour force, 20,000 solicitors was a happy solution to an otherwise discouraging problem. Solicitors are similar in social and educational background to their Bar colleagues. Cross-sections will be found to go to the same schools and universities and to have the same interests. Many of them become highly expert as lawyers, and a few have been distinguished as profound and even great lawyers. They are spread throughout the country so that a reasonable assortment is available in every area.

As a profession they have furnished a Prime Minister, a couple of Chancellors of the Exchequer, two or three Home Secretaries and an endless list of other public offices. Of course great numbers would be unsuitable for the judiciary, and some who were suitable would not want such appointment, but on a simple statistical basis if 20,000 of the same sort of people are added to the existing 2,000 it is a near statistical certainty that the new and enlarged pool will throw up ten times as many likely choices.

No one can deny the incongruity of denying solicitors the right to act as judges in County Courts where for decades they have discharged the overwhelming burden of advocacy, and the equal incongruity of a proposal – nakedly designed to maintain a monopoly of dubious public benefit – whereby solicitors shall only be admitted as advocates in the new courts where the Lord Chancellor is satisfied that there are insufficient barristers to discharge the duties. Again it is merciful not to dissect this proposition.

The English Bench has, and maintains, a great tradition. It is not because it is drawn from the Bar but because this country breeds men of outstanding judicial quality and learning. The extension of the gathering ground to include solicitors (and, I would fervently hope, academic lawyers of whom a number are wholly suitable) will do nothing to injure that tradition, but will maintain its strength unimpaired. Nothing but good can come from enlarging the choice of judges to include men with daily experience of their fellow human beings in their natural surroundings.

(*The Times*, November 19, 1970)

6. *The City of London Court*

The test we apply in this country is a valuable and valid test – whether an institution works. And by the test of whether it works, the City of London Court has an enormously strong position. No one has argued – no one can argue – that this has not been a most successful court. The statistics about the cases that have been before the court were given by the noble and learned Lord, the Lord Chief Justice, on Second Reading. I will refresh your Lordships' memories and repeat these figures, for the sake of noble Lords who did not happen to be here on Second Reading, because they are so impressive.

In the last year for which records are available, 19,000 cases came before this court. Leaving aside a few cases that were referred, on case stated, to the Divisional Court or other higher Court, the cases that were heard on appeal were twenty in number, of which six were successful. So this court has a record of having tried 19,000 cases, of which the decisions in only six were reversed by an appellate tribunal. It is difficult to believe that any court anywhere in this country could achieve a better result than that. If we were to judge the matter by normal criteria we should really be down on our bended knees begging the

City aldermen to continue in office. We should not be advancing highly theoretical reasons why their court should be abolished.

Two things were said in the course of the Second Reading debate on which I ought to comment. One was that the City has done a good deal of lobbying in this matter; and that was said with some sense of reproach, as if it was wrong for them to do so. I think that they would have been open to reproach if they had not done so. If the City believe so strongly as they do in the value of their court, then they are quite right to lobby and to seek every legitimate means they can to preserve an institution by which they set special value.

The second thing said, which does them much less than justice, was that the whole of this matter resolved itself into the question of whether the City aldermen are prepared to demean themselves by sitting on the bench with ordinary human beings. If I may say so, I think that is an unworthy representation of the whole position. Nobody who knows the City aldermen will believe that that is the matter which concerns them. What concerns them is that they want to preserve a traditional court as part of the whole fabric of the City by which they set great store. What we shall be doing, if we abolish this court, is to tug at one string of a whole tapestry of tradition, and if we do that we shall be impairing and endangering the whole tapestry. I think that that is the real danger of the proposal.

Should we do this? Here is a court that is held in high repute by every branch of the legal profession. The Bar regard it highly. The judiciary have already come to your Lordships' House to testify how highly they esteem this court, and no doubt they will speak again this afternoon. I think that no member of the judiciary, except the most lofty member of it, has expressed an opinion adverse or contrary to the standing of this court. The solicitors' profession, through the Law Society, has also expressed its approval of the court. The Magistrates' Association has said that, whatever views may be held about *ex officio* justices of the peace generally, they do not apply to the Mayor and aldermen of the City.

On every side where informed opinion exists there is the view that this court ought to survive. There is even, implicitly and by inference, the approval of the defendants before the court. I have never seen a letter in any newspaper – nor heard of any complaint by anyone tried before this court – that he had an unfair trial because he became before one alderman and there were not three justices sitting there to try him. I cannot believe that if such a feeling had been widespread over the years it would not have been expressed by the people who have actually been tried in this court. I think that one is entitled to say, therefore, that there is total satisfaction on all sides by all concerned with the administration of justice in this court, including the accused.

On one side, we have a court that is regarded as entirely satisfactory, free from any possible complaint; and, on the other, we have the contention that it is an anomaly. And what are the reasons why it is regarded as an anomaly? I think that they are best found in some of the speeches made in another place. I do not discount those reasons or speeches, but in my view they add up to nothing like sufficient to redress the balance against the weight of overwhelming opinion in favour of the court's survival.

First, it is said that no women sit on the court. There seems to be some view that there is a woman somewhere within the aldermanic structure slowly forcing her way to the top. I do not know whether the lady has arrived at this moment, or when she is likely to become an alderman. I have no wish to make the slightest use of this sort of argument. I would say squarely that there are no women. But I make the point to the noble and learned Lord, the Lord Chancellor, that there are many legal courts where women do not feature predominantly. He will go down in history as the first Lord Chancellor to appoint a woman as a High Court Judge. This stands to his credit; but, so far as I know, only one such woman has been appointed, and any High Court Judge who is looking for a female companionship will have to look far and wide before he encounters it in the Divorce Division.

If we look for something to reform in relation to the absence of women, then the Chancery Division is eminently the place to look, for there we find infancy cases, wardship cases, cases where it is eminently necessary – indeed, imperative – that the opinions of women are sought. Yet they never are sought. So far as judicial opinion is concerned, there is no woman in the Chancery Court. Let us hasten to reform that and put some women in the Chancery Division before we start knocking about the Lord Mayor and aldermen of the City of London. I venture to think that this is not a very convincing argument.

The cases that do require women – cases of juvenile delinquency and matrimonial cases – are few in number, because the City is not a dormitory area. The City is a place where people conduct business, and matrimonial disputes rarely arise in the course of stockbroking activities. The City contrives not to have these matters to deal with. There is a trifling number in the course of a year and they could conveniently be passed to an adjoining court that has the requisite personnel to deal with them. The same is true of juvenile delinquency. The City does not produce an atmosphere which encourages juvenile delinquency. Juvenile delinquents go off elsewhere for their unhappy activities.

So far as the City Court is concerned, there is this to be said: that, having no women, it contrives to produce a better record of successes than the courts which have women. It may be a sad fact for feminists to reflect on (I am almost terrified to say this with some of the company present here this afternoon), but it is the fact that if you look at the records of courts throughout the country where there are women on the bench, you find that they do not add up to the record that I have just given your Lordships – that is, of only six successful appeals out of 19,000 cases. Therefore we have no logical reason to suppose that if we were to change this court to have women, we should achieve any better results. The logic and statistics, indeed, establish that we should achieve even worse results.

The other argument advanced is that this court consists of a single magistrate sitting on his own; and it is said that this is a bad thing. But, of course, all the stipendiary magistrates sit on their own; they are single magistrates. Judges sit on their own. Where is this sort of argument to stop? No one has ever suggested that a stipendiary magistrate should be reinforced by two lay justices because he is sitting by himself. We shall be told, of course, that he is a trained lawyer. I, as a lawyer, can say that I believe that lawyers are no more immune from prejudices than anyone else. I have at times encountered some who are more prone to prejudices than others. I certainly should not regard it as a valid argument that a man may sit alone because he is a lawyer. I hope we shall not hear that suggested; but if it is, I hope that it will not be accepted.

The third argument that is put forward is a startling argument — what I call the levelling argument: that there are no working-class people sitting on the City bench. I do not know what is meant by 'working-class'. I think it has a very elastic meaning. Do we mean a person who started in poor and humble circumstances and has remained there? Do we mean a person who started in poor and humble circumstances and improved himself, and perhaps has become an alderman of the City? If we mean the latter, there are certainly such people on the bench. If we mean the former, certainly not; and I do not know that the bench is any the worse for not having them. All I would say is that it would be a startling thing to introduce these theoretical considerations in order to destroy such a validly established institution.

I think the City Court exists as an anomaly. But it is a most valuable anomaly, and it has justified its existence thousands of times over. Why does the City want to preserve it? I am not going to make a long speech, because I believe everything that has to be said on this subject has already been said, but I think it is important to say a few words on the subject of the City's tradition. At this moment, if I may say so, we should all be very concerned about the preservation of traditions. When we see the things that are happening all over the world, and indeed in some parts of this country, because of the absence of tradition; when we see the uncertainties that are introduced into the masses of young people who have no traditions to guide them, no historic principles by which they are led, I wonder whether we are so wise to demolish traditions with such carefree abandon as we are minded to do in this case.

The City is not seeking for privilege as an inherited right. The City is not saying: 'We want the privilege of administering justice because we were born to it.' The City is seeking for the privilege to discharge duties; it is seeking for the privilege of retaining rights to which people come over a long graduation of hard work, civil distinction and sacrifice, with an enormous amount of time and effort. I do not think this is a right of which they should be deprived. I think people should be encouraged to retain this sort of privilege. This is the best sort of privilege. It is not open to a shred of objection.

In using the word 'City' we are, I think, minded to confuse the great throbbing commercial centre, where people are exchanging share prices, floating companies, selling sterling short, long or whatever they are doing with it, with a community of people in the City who are dedicated to public work – the people of whom we are talking today. The aldermen of the City are appointed by a democratic process. They are voted for by the ratepayers. Having been elected by the ratepayers, they are confirmed by their own body, which means, as I think the Lord Chief Justice said, that every City magistrate is confirmed by a panel of twenty-six or so other magistrates. It seems to me to be an entirely democratic system of appointment. I can see that theoretical objections can be raised to it, but it has a democratic basis; it is a democratic way of appointing them.

What is the doctrinaire system for which we are to change this? If there were some splendid system that we had devised that was preferable; if we were going to knock down this court because the system to be adopted throughout the country was so excellent in itself that no one could raise the faintest objection to it, there might be an argument even against the powerful arguments which I think we have already heard on this. But what is the system? The reason why we are told that this is an anomaly, and that democracy demands that we destroy this court, is a system whereby every magistrate is nominated by a political officer. This is the system that we are asked to adopt. It is no use concealing the fact that it is a system that has worked over the years. But the whole system of judicial patronage, the whole system of judicial appointment in this country, works because we have people of exceptional personal quality. It does not work because it is a system that is good on its own. No one can say that it is a good system to have one man nominating everybody.

Some while back I ventured to ask the noble and learned Lord the Lord Chancellor how he came to appoint the judges – what method was employed. He, of course, nominates all the justices of the peace. With quiet modesty, if I may say so, he admitted that he also appointed all the judges, and he seemed rather puzzled that anyone should raise any suggestion that this was not the best way of doing things. But I think that we do need to look at these things very closely. We are not opposing to the system in the City a system that speaks for itself and is self-evidently to be preferred. We are opposing to it a system that has worked, over the years, simply because we have had the good fortune to have Lord Chancellors of exceptional quality, and because the whole of the Bar, as we all know, is an institution of total integrity. But it does not work because it has theoretical advantages. The anomaly, if I may say so, is the method that we are adopting elsewhere, not the method that we are seeking to adopt in the City.

It is for this reason – it is not a political matter – that I venture to ask your Lordships to think very hard whether we should destroy this ancient institution; whether we should destroy the opportunity of rendering the services that the aldermen of the City and the Lord Mayor have asked for, in face of the alleged theoretical advantage which, when it is examined, is seen not to be there at all.

I think the City were entirely right to lobby as hard as they could to preserve their court. When this matter was raised in another place one Member said, I think, that having studied the City he could not discover any aldermen of Labour or Liberal persuasion. This I know to be totally wrong. There is one Member of your Lordships' House who is of Labour persuasion, and is an alderman. I do not know what are the political opinions of the present Lord Mayor, but I should have to go a long way to find a more liberally-minded man. It does not seem to me that the question is: What are the politics of the aldermen? The question is: If I were an accused person, should I be safe in their hands? And my feeling is that I should feel entirely safe in the hands of the aldermen whom I have met in the City. If justice responds to that test, then I think it is good justice; and I think that we should be treading on very dangerous ground indeed, and should be showing great temerity, if we were to destroy a great institution which achieves results of this kind simply because it is thought there are theoretical benefits to be gained on account of some theory of uniformity. I do ask your Lordships, when my Amendment comes to be moved, to support it, on the simple ground that there is here something that works well, and that the reasons advanced for destroying it are totally specious.

(Speech in the House of Lords, May 13, 1968)

7. *The Biafran War (I)*

My Lords, I believe that we have pursued a disastrously mistaken policy. But I believe also that there is still an opportunity to rectify it. I do not believe that the people who have carried out that policy are criminals, with bloodstained hands. I believe that they are honourable, well-meaning people, who are as humane as anyone in this House, and certainly as humane as I am. But I believe that they were totally mistaken, and that their mistake arises from error, and also perhaps from the least forgivable attribute, that of obstinacy. I believe that they have declined to look at the facts that are staring them in the face.

There were three demonstrations, relatively simple ones, of how Her Majesty's Government and their spokesman here today have swallowed, totally uncritically and without question, everything that comes out of Federal Nigeria. First of all, there was the unedifying situation with regard to the construction of the speech made by General Gowon on television yesterday. That speech was open to only one interpretation. There was no possible element of doubt about what he meant; no gloss can be put upon it; nobody can refine it or adjust it or adapt it so that it fits into our comfortable preconceptions of what the policy is. The man has said in the clearest possible terms that he is going to force the fight to an issue. He has said that in my hearing. If there is one thing that I have come to trust over the years, my Lords, it is the reliability of my own hearing. When I cease to trust that, I shall cease to function in any capacity. I heard him say it on television, and other Members of your Lordships' House heard General Gowon say it. It cannot be explained away.

Then there were the reassuring utterances about what General Gowon was going to do when he got into the hot land of the Ibo. Not a word was said about the bloodcurdling utterances of his leader, the gentleman who has been announcing that he is going to shoot at anything that moves. The noble Lord, Lord Hunt, to whom the whole of this House and the whole of the country is deeply indebted for having undertaken that thankless mission, said that the General was nothing more than a public school type. Those of us here may well think that that is what the General is, and we might come to regard him as a very agreeable and pleasant fellow to have a drink with in a club. But when you think of the cowering, terrified masses in Biafra, I am afraid that they will not construe these statements in that way. They will construe them quite literally. They will say: 'This man intends to murder us.' Not a word has been said on that subject by Her Majesty's Government.

And, if I may say so, most facile of all were the explanations of the various negotiations for peace treaties. These negotiations, in my opinion, have been totally and utterly valueless, because they have been directed towards an impossibility. They have throughout been restricted to formal and procedural considerations. In London they argued about where the peace discussions were to take place, about what the agenda was to be, and about whether they were to have a chairman – and in fact they departed without a chairman. A greater absurdity it is impossible to imagine, than these two adversaries confronting each other across the peace table without an independent chairman. But that is not what the London discussions were about.

Then they went to Kampala, and many of your Lordships may have read the record of the proceedings in Kampala, as written about by Sir Louis Mbanafo. I should like to say a word about Sir Louis Mbanafo. I have known him for most of my life; we were undergraduates together. If there is one man I would trust, it is that man. If there is one man whose opinion I would take, it is that man's. My concern and interest in the Biafran situation arises simply from my friendship with him. I have met over the years many other of the Biafran leaders. But I believe what he says, and he gave me an account of the Kampala negotiations that made it quite clear that the Federal Government were treading a stately minuet; that there was no genuine or sincere desire on anyone's part to achieve a settlement that involved a cease-fire. And, if I may say so, one cannot blame them, because each side wanted something quite different.

The Biafrans wanted a cease-fire because they were losing the war; a cease-fire would be a military advantage to them; it would relieve the military pressure. The Federal Government did not want a cease-fire: they wanted a capitulation. And the two people were negotiating for objectives to which they gave the same term, the same description, but which were totally different things. All the negotiations had been concerned with these preliminaries, preliminaries which could never achieve a result because the vital and essential matter with which we should have concerned ourselves – which was first to arrive at a constitutional settlement that would be acceptable to both sides – has, deplorably enough, never been discussed under our aegis or under our auspices with both sides present, or even without that intermediary.

Why is this so? The explanation is that we have for some reason adopted the view that the Federal Government of Nigeria is a legal government and the Biafran Government is an illegal government, a rebel government. Nigeria was granted its independence in 1960. It was granted a Federal Constitution after the most careful and anxious thought by this country. No one can be blamed. There were commissions, minority commissions, that went out to consider whether there should be three or four areas. There were discussions about whether there should be a Middle West tribe. The Willinck Commission considered the whole matter and decided in favour of three territories, and a Federal Government was granted.

I think that that form of government was in itself incapable of achieving a successful result, for the simple reason that it created a division of the territory which ensured that in each of the three territories there was one dominant tribe, and no possibility at all that any one of the tribes could achieve a majority throughout the integrated territory. That was the built-in situation created by the constitution which we granted. It was adjusted subsequently when a fourth territory was created, contrary to the recommendations of the Willinck Commission, by the creation of a Mid-West territory following the grant of independence.

Then in 1963 (I do not think this matter was mentioned by the Minister) there was of course the creation of a Republic, and the creation of a further constitution, and Nigeria became fully independent as a Republican Constitution. At that stage legal government existed in Nigeria. One knew where it was; one knew where to find it. Then came the *coups*. In January, 1966, there came the first of the *coups*. What I believe were called the 'Ibo majors' massacred the Prime Minister and a number of other people. It was, I have no doubt, a highly reprehensible matter. It was not a purely tribal matter, and it was significant that the massacre was put down by an army leader who was himself an Ibo. It was significant that the Quartermaster General at that time, himself an Ibo, was shot dead because he refused to hand over arms and ammunitions to the rebels.

Thus it was quite clear that this was not a division along purely tribal lines. But the fact remains that there was an insurrection largely inspired by the Ibos. That came in January, 1966, and at that stage the Cabinet, as I understand it, apprehensive of the continuation of democratic or legal government in civil form, asked General Ironsi if he would take over the Government and conduct it in a state of emergency.

At that stage, I should have thought, there ceased to be a constitutional legal government as we understand it. At that stage there was an *ad hoc* government operating because it exercised control in a certain territory. But, further, there came the second *coup* in June or July, 1966, when Ironsi was murdered and when, following a period of very considerable confusion, as I understand it, Colonel Gowon emerged as the leader. Colonel Gowon was not even, in terms of seniority, the lineal successor to Ironsi. He was several stages removed in seniority, but he was the person who assumed power. How can it remotely be suggested by any legal authority that his Government has the status of a legal government? Yet we have stated this blandly and blindly; iterated it and reiterated it to a point where it has dominated all our thinking in this matter, and where, if I may say so, it has directed the whole of our policy, to the extent where we have imposed upon ourselves a total paralysis in any useful action. Because by saying that we are dealing with a legal government that was not a legal government, we have of course said that we cannot deal with anyone else.

The situation arises – and I do not profess to be an international lawyer; it may be that the Government will produce arguments to dispute this – that there are two *ad hoc* legal governments in existence in the Nigerian territory at the moment. There is the Gowon Government – or was – which *ad hoc* and *de facto* controlled an area of territory, because it was operating it and controlling it effectively; and there was the Biafran area – whatever portion of that was in fact controlled by Colonel Ojukwu. That appears to me to be the legal situation. But not only is that the legal situation, but that is the situation to which we should have cleaved with enthusiasm, because that gave us an opportunity of doing something effective. I am by no means sure that the aspirations of the Biafrans towards total independence can ever be achieved. I am by no means sure that they take sufficiently into account the economic considerations and considerations of the minority. But what I am absolutely convinced of is that if we had effectively negotiated between these people on the basis that they both had *ad hoc* governments, we could have arrived at some compromise for a loose confederation that would have been acceptable to them both.

I have had long, almost endless, discussions with Biafran leaders. I have put innumerable permutations and alternatives to them about what sort of government might be a possibility within a confederation. I have had, personally, a most encouraging response. They have frequently said to me, 'Yes, this might be a possibility. But how do we ensure, pray, that if we are attacked, we can defend ourselves?' Because, if I may say so, Her Majesty's Minister this morning did less than justice to the real apprehensions of the Ibos and of the Easterners, because not only Ibos are concerned. He said very little about the fact that they fled back to their territory after a massacre. One does not want to make too much of it, but they have it fully in mind, constantly in mind. Their solitary recollection is that 20,000, 30,000 or 40,000 of them – I do not know how many, but nobody has ever put the figure at less than 20,000 – were in fact massacred in the North. It was, I think, a little unworthy that the Government should have suggested that there was a justification for this because there was a general apprehension that the Ibos were about to seize power. Supposing there was such an apprehension. Could that remotely have justified such a course?

Just think what we could have done to reassure them had we remained in dialogue with them. But we cut ourselves totally off from dialogue. We offered them no reassurance; we never said to them that these people were not going to murder them. We never said: 'We will see to it that you are not murdered; international forces will see that you are not murdered.' General Gowon is a nice civilized man, as has been said, and I do not deny it for a moment. The fact remains that this is not believed in Biafra, and if people tell me that the Biafrans are fighting because of notions of aggrandisement or because they want oil, or for any other reason, I tell them simply that that is not the case. Whatever the ambitions of Colonel Ojukwu may have been, the simple fact is that at this moment of time the Biafrans – the simple people in Biafra – are fighting because they believe that if they give up the fight they will be massacred. That is their belief; it may be a mistaken belief, but it is a belief and an anxiety that we had it within our power to allay.

When I started to speak I said that I thought there was something constructive still to be done. This remains my belief. I believe that we should put ourselves into touch with the Biafran chiefs. I believe that we should allay the anxiety and suspicion about us that exists in Biafra – and that principally because of the dispatch of arms. It is not that we were under any obligation to dispatch arms. A more extraordinary proposition I do not think has ever been enunciated in international law. Allowing even that this was a legal State could we then in any circumstances be under an immutable and absolute obligation to supply arms for whatever use they wanted to put them to?

How does such an obligation ever arise, and when has it arisen before? I say, and I assert most positively, that this is not a legal

State. This is a State that had no claim on any footing; and if it was a legal State this is an untenable claim for a legal State to make. But the damage of the supply of arms was not whether or not they would have got them from somewhere else, but that it shattered the confidence of the Biafrans in the British, because there is no territory in the whole of Africa where British authority sounded deeper and sounded richer than it did in Biafra before this war started.

Men like Mbanafo and his colleagues were anglophiles to the last of their breath. They were educated in England. Here was a man created a knight by Her Majesty and made the Chief Justice of Eastern Nigeria. His colleagues were wholly dedicated to the British cause. We forfeited the whole of that because of this imbecile persistence in supplying arms, and if the Nigerians could have got the arms from somewhere else, good luck to them. If we believed that the Nigerians ought to win the war, and knew also that they could win the war by getting the arms from somewhere else, well let them get them from somewhere else. But why should we have forfeited confidence, why should we have alienated the good will, why should we have created and maintained disaffection when it was going to do this irreparable damage?

I believe that everything that has been done has been done with the best of intentions and in the belief that it is right, but alas! hell and Biafra are paved with good intentions. Even at this late hour I urge the Government to reconsider. I think the Government still can do something effective, but they must reconsider their policy, and reconsider it in the light of reality and not concern themselves with the question of what propaganda is coming out of Biafra.

How pitiful, if I may say so, that a Minister of the Crown should concern himself with the question of what stories were being put about and believed by poor, cowed, terrified creatures in Biafra, whether they believed that a football team was an army or not. If I were a native in Biafra whose child was starving, who was being subjected to bombardment, whose relatives were being murdered all around, I would believe absolutely any rumour and report that I was told. If I may say so, having at times found myself in England during the war, I well remember the rumours and reports that were believed by quite sensible people in this country at that time. There was no story too extravagant for some people to believe. But what a thing to reproach them with! If I may venture to say so, if they are defending themselves by propaganda, then it is the clamant cries of a man sinking for the third time. Those cries may be very offensive indeed to civilized ears, but it is the only form of hope that is still open to the poor wretched creatures.

I venture to ask the Government to think very long before they pursue a policy that I am convinced can end only in disaster. I am absolutely convinced of the complete authenticity of everything the noble Viscount said – that there is no military solution to this problem at all. If the Ibo are defeated – if the Easterners are defeated, because I do not accept the story that the whole of the rest of the eastern tribes are not fighting with them; it is completely inconsistent with the fact that the war has been maintained for this length of time, and people who come out of Biafra do not support it – and these people take to the bush, heaven knows what disaster will descend upon the whole of Africa.

I would echo what the noble Viscount said to Colonel Ojukwu. If his position stands in the way of a settlement, then it is an enormous responsibility for one man to assume that he should allow his personal ambitions and hopes and notions to imperil the lives of the whole of his people. I have not met Colonel Ojukwu. I earnestly hope that he will give heed to these words, and that if there is a possibility of a settlement that involves compromising the maximum hopes and aspirations of the Biafrans, that the Biafrans, like everyone else, will listen to sense. But I am sure that even today we have a mediating role, and this is the role we should immediately undertake.

(Speech in the House of Lords, August 27, 1968)

8. The Biafran War (II)

No one, not even a supporter of the Government's Nigerian policy, could read this book without revulsion and horror. Unhappily such supporters will read it with the same total myopia as has induced a policy which – taking the kindest view – shares responsibility for a situation which many profound experts on the subject believe could have been terminated long ago, had wiser and more humane considerations prevailed in this country.

The book contains an adequate exposition of the background and a full statement of the political factors operating both in this country and in the United States. They do not make agreeable reading. Briefly it is a story of the apparent determination of a great part of the so-called civilized world to destroy a people of dauntless courage and tenacity whose solitary crime is that they are opposed to the constitutional doctrine of federation. It is doubtful whether in human history legalism has been extended to more demented lengths.

How, therefore, has it been possible for honest and honourable men – for indeed they are this – to argue themselves into a belief that their policy is not only justifiable but right? The reasons advanced are complicated, but the real causes, I think, are simple. Basically I believe that the Biafran policy conducted in this country would have been different had anyone able to exercise real power understood the problem. Instead, busy ministers beset with innumerable other problems not unnaturally decided that this remote and seemingly limited conflict did not justify an immense amount of concentrated study. It was very much a case of accepting the opinion of the local advisers. The recommendations that came to the British Government – and to which they have clung with the obstinacy of suicidal limpets ever since – were that the Nigerian Federation should be maintained from the outset, because the war would be a short one and it would be madness to alienate the goodwill of the inevitable victors.

This appalling blunder of judgment has been at the root of the whole catastrophic British approach to the matter, and it was not even an excusable error. Independent Nigerian experts had issued solemn warnings that it would not be a short war; that the Ibos had a will and power to resist that no one should underrate, but since the British Government listen to no voices but the official voice, and designated all other viewpoints as expressions of academic and partisan eccentricity, no second and rational assessment was taken of the situation in realistic power terms.

At the outset, the Government's argument was that the supply of arms would maintain its authority with the Federation to enable it to organize a just peace – the nature of its justice being left vague and undefined. It is terrifying that we could continue to maintain these assertions in the light of the proposals for Biafra contained in the twelve-state plan of the Nigerian government, which had only to be inspected for a second to see that the promise of just treatment to the Ibos and other eastern tribes was a simple lie. Nor was the matter made any better by the dark and sinister suggestions that if we ceased to supply the arms the Russians would seize the opportunity, and by doing so would supplant our authority, a matter of pure and unevidenced conjecture. As the conflict developed the British Government's policy became more nakedly partisan. The supply of arms is now being effected quite simply to achieve the total defeat and capitulation of the Biafrans.

We were at first told that our obligation to supply arms arose from the fact that the Federal Government was a legal government. I and others challenged this impossible contention in the Lords, and pointed out that if anything it was one stage further removed from legality than the Biafran Government of Colonel Ojukwu. I noticed some hasty consultations on Government benches and not a whisper of a reply. But a second and more plausible ploy was that we were the time-honoured suppliers – the traditional suppliers – of arms to Nigeria, and that the situation was rather akin to an honest and reliable greengrocer failing to provide the cauliflower in time for Sunday lunch. It was no business of the greengrocer to inquire about the guests who would consume it. It was none of our business to ask the purpose for which our weapons would be used.

And so the unhappy story has proceeded. It is of very little importance to the victims whether the decision was made by an honest man acting in folly or a man actuated by more devious and calculating motives. It is a more frightening prospect for the world if a Biafra can be brought about through muddle and ignorance and arrogance and obstinacy in men who, on any personal assessment, would be models of domestic morality.

(Review of *Biafra: Britain's Shame*, by Auberon Waugh and Suzanne Cronje – Michael Joseph, *Spectator*, November 8, 1969)

PART THREE

The Arts

1. *In Place of Censors*

In June 1967, the Joint Committee on Censorship of the Theatre – appointed by the then Home Secretary, Roy Jenkins – produced a report of commendable brevity, emphasis and unanimity. The unanimity was mildly surprising, since the committee contained among its members an ex-Lord Chamberlain, a former Conservative Home Secretary and Lord Chancellor (who died in the course of its procedure and was replaced by another Conservative ex-Home Secretary) and certainly a couple of other members who would not have been expected wholeheartedly to support the total abolition of pre-censorship of plays and the total abrogation of the Lord Chamberlain's functions in the theatre. Yet, to the delight of the creative theatre, of writers, directors, and of the more progressive managements, the report was unqualified in its recommendation that it was an unwarranted interference with liberty of thought and speech for a theatrical presentation to be proscribed from production without the prior approval of a public official.

The report was the culmination of a battle that had waxed for many years. The topic had consistently provoked interest to a point of indignation and had four times been considered by Parliamentary committees. In hearings by the 1909 Committee, feeling and vehemence were expressed by a flood of witnesses: not merely dramatists but distinguished novelists, artists and a multitude of creative persons came to testify to the affront that the existence of the Lord Chamberlain put upon creative writing. If for nothing else the proceedings were immortalized in Bernard Shaw's famous description of his own attendance before the Committee and the hubbub when he was handed back his printed memoranda.

The 1966 Committee received evidence which, so far as it was rendered orally, was sparse in number and almost uniform in character. But it did not lack excitement or entertainment, usually hinged on moments when it was investigating not the abolition of pre-censorship of plays – which was taken almost for granted from the outset – but possible safeguards to management. One such was a voluntary system of censorship, a course recommended by the 1909 Committee (which, in justice, had itself as its main recommendation called for the abolition of the censorship).

Those in the 1966 Committee who might have supported the principle of voluntary censorship – which would have allowed a play to be produced without licence, but gave a choice to a manager or dramatist to elect for the security of a voluntary licence – were, like myself, persuaded by the evidence that this compromise solution was unacceptable within the profession as a whole; and although I must confess to a faint hankering for the experiment, I adopted the wise precept that 'it is better to think yourself mad than the rest of the world mistaken', and that a total absence of supporters for a scheme argues its shortcomings.

The report of the Committee has not yet been enshrined in Government legislation, but the Chairman of the Committee, Mr G. R. Strauss, M.P., who conducted its affairs with efficiency and impartiality, is introducing the substance of the report in a Private Member's Bill this session. In view of the unanimity of the report the Bill deserves full Government backing, and it is to be hoped will pass through both Houses. It would be a legitimate reproach in democratic affairs if the unanimous opinion of a wholly representative committee did not emerge on the statute book.

But one or two afterthoughts are very relevant, particularly in consequence of the recent 'Last Exit to Brooklyn' decision at the Old Bailey. Those who, like myself, were canvassing the possibility of a voluntary system, were not concerned with the dangers to public morality which might arise from removing restrictions on freedom of production. To a man, we regarded this as an acceptable risk which would in any event be controlled 'more than adequately' by the obscenity laws to which the stage was now to conform. The emphasis is on 'more than adequately'. Our fear was that the removal of censorship would produce not a more liberal but a less liberal theatre, with managements inhibited by the fear of prosecutions and, deprived of the insurance of a Lord Chamberlain's licence, adopting a policy of greater timidity: that plays now and previously presented in the West End and elsewhere would not see the light of day – which, with the recent decision restricting the operation of club theatres, might mean that effectively they would be produced not at all. It must be understood that this risk was fully manifest during the proceedings of the Committee; in reaching their decision the Committee took cognisance of it, and quite deliberately opted for a free theatre, no Lord Chamberlain and – coupled with this historical emancipation – the risk that natural prudence, if not timidity, on the part of the managements, would present difficulties to adventurous dramatists.

The 'Last Exit' decision has, of course, reinforced the misgivings of those who do not regard the ordinary processes of prosecution, and the ordinary prosecuting authorities, as appropriate to deal with matters of the mind. This is not the place to argue again the 'Last Exit' case, though in my opinion by no literate standards was the work obscene. The decision was arrived at by what is described as 'the robust common sense of juries' and not by literate standards. What caused the damage was one simple fact: that a jury – whatever its robust common sense – could not fail to ask itself why one book out of hundreds of thousands found itself pilloried the dock at the Old Bailey. From this damaging vantage-point only a classic like 'Lady Chatterly', written by an author long dead and of immense and increasing international renown, had any comfortable prospect of acquittal.

The moral of the 'Last Exit' case is not that the Lord Chamberlain's departure should be delayed (and in saying this it would be wrong not to pay tribute to the enlightened exercise of his office by the present incumbent) but to ensure that the legislation recommended in broad principle in the Committee's report should obviate major risks to the theatre. A parallel provision should be enacted for literature, whose present censorship dilemma has been brought into such conspicuous relief by the unhappy fate of 'Last Exit'.

Two safeguards, I think, are important: first and absolutely foremost, that no book or play should be prosecuted without the approval of a literate official or body such as an *ad hoc* Home Office Committee specially selected for the purpose. The proposal by the Joint Committee was that the prior approval of the Attorney General should be sought; but many lawyers might consider that this is not a function in which legal qualifications have special relevance, and that a committee of literary and other experts is to be preferred. Second, a requirement which should, I think, be antecedent to any prosecution of a play or book: notice of the matters complained of in the play or book must be served before any such prosecution is launched. The management or publisher should be entitled to discuss the notice with the prosecuting authority; and if so minded (but only if so minded) make appropriate changes which would in ordinary circumstances debar prosecution.

There is manifestly no perfect solution to this problem. Pre-censorship of books would today be a totally unthinkable notion. Voluntary censorship is rejected by most of the thinking elements in the professions concerned. If, therefore, the matter is to be left to the post-censorship of the courts it is of cardinal importance to writers, managers and publishers alike that ill-judged prosecutions (the cost of which must be forbidding and may be ruinous) are avoided by sensible preliminary safeguards.

(Sunday Times, January 21, 1968)

2. Arts Council Reports, 1967–70: The Chairman's Introduction

1967

Although the Arts Council is now a well-established institution, its policy and working methods are by no means fully evolved. The additional resources – given to us by a Government anxious to stimulate and develop the work we do – have emphasized the problems and difficulties that confront us.

The major problem is to define our scope. We remain and always will remain an auxiliary body. Artistic activity would, happily, continue without us, and the contribution we can make to promoting artistic output will always be arguable. On this score we take a modest view. We have no evidence that poets, authors, painters or composers – or any creative workers – are the more fertile because we exist and give them our support. It would be complacent to entertain such beliefs. But that does not detract from the relevance of a body with a function to improve the working conditions of artists and to preserve and enlarge their public.

For it is this latter function that constitutes our major activity, and the highest service that we can render to the artist. And it is to this objective that the bulk of our resources and energies have been and will continue to be devoted.

There are few thinking people to whom the need for artistic subsidy would have to be justified today. It is not a matter of choice. In some ways, it might be preferable to live in a society where the measure of private support for our activities obviated the need for State assistance. But such a society has totally ceased to exist. The fiscal policies of every government in our memory have contributed to a situation where private bounty or investment is now totally inadequate to sustain a civilized ration of music and theatre, of poetry and pictures. Nor need we be remotely apologetic in asking for the modest sums we need for our purposes from the public purse. The Government has garnered in much, if not most, of the wealth that cultured patricians and public-spirited industrialists could formerly bestow. It holds a portion of its treasury charged with a trust to use it for our purposes – and, in fairness, the growth of the Arts Council in scope and importance demonstrates governmental recognition of this principle.

We have, we believe, started to evolve a firm policy – and the pages of this report furnish some guide to it. But it must be protean. We do not exist to plan artistic and cultural projects. Very few are the fruit of direct Arts Council labours. And this is as it should be. The larger the extent of national subsidy, the more vital that it should neither bear nor seem to bear the imprint of a single body. Artistic life in this country must not be dominated by a small, non-elected, appointed caucus in St James's Square. The avoidance even of the possibility of such domination is a conscious plank of our policy. Thus we encourage local plans and promotions; thus we encourage the development of a sensible regionalism – not the 'fragmentation' of established important institutions or the notion that every town must have an opera house, but the support of the thesis that in a great and closely populated country it is an absurdity that every major artistic institution should be crowded into the metropolis. We recognize with humility the magnitude of our problems. How shall we reconcile the diffusion of money and effort with the maintenance of quality? How can we find enough money to promote important new ventures without danger to those already established and entitled to a legitimate growth factor? How can we find, train, and support the new administrators upon whom the whole operation depends? Over the years we have made an active and tangible contribution to the scene. But certainly not alone. And this is welcome. The contribution of the BBC to the spread and quality of British music is epochal. There are great areas for collaboration. The English Theatre flourished under private management before we were dreamed of. It is our duty, in the administration of subsidy, to co-operate with its best elements. Whether we can or should in the end give direct aid to private managements is a problem we are now investigating.

For we are determined, so far as our facilities permit, to find out the facts and legislate on as sensibly an informed basis as we can contrive. We have set up – and shall shortly hear from – a strong inquiry into the needs of opera and ballet throughout the nation. We have just appointed an equally strong committee of inquiry (under the chairmanship of Sir William Emrys Williams) into the needs of drama. We have, adventurously, appointed a statistician. We shall try to make our judgments more scientific and less rule-of-thumb, to a large extent they must remain inspirational – others might find a less flattering word.

There is a great deal of challenging work to do. We do it – I believe healthily – in an atmosphere of active and even vigorous debate. We are conscious of the enormous power we wield over the lives of many people and organizations. We endeavour to discharge our duties with a very real consciousness of our own fallibility and the rooted imperfection of artistic judgment. And as a Council we have the boon of a directorate and staff which, in its work, daily demonstrates the belief that it is serving a cause.

1968

Once again, much emphasis is on the regions or, more accurately, on those parts of Great Britain outside London. London presents a special problem: it is foolish to regard it as sufficiently served by artistic and cultural amenities to a point where it can now be neglected in favour of other areas, but simple justice compels us to call a relative halt to expansion in many London plans and institutions until at least something comparable to the London 'density' of culture is available in other parts of the country.

We must recognize – as we have over the years – that there is a considerable element of inconsistency in the distribution of the good things in the world of theatre, art and music in different towns and in different countries. In part, this is due to history and the accident of population distribution, the location of industry and the concentration of the other requisite elements to create a demand; but we have always conceded that in part it is due to our deliberate policy of deferring to local requirements as they arise, and only in very rare cases seeking to stimulate some local activity where at least the nucleus of existing demand is not already established. I believe this policy to be basically right. I do not believe that, with the immense present demand that exists in various localities, any other policy is a possibility; but it may be that, as time goes on, we will have to consider a change, and it was with this very much in mind that we decided on the appointment of a regional adviser to give more detailed and systematic consideration to regional planning, not merely from London but in conjunction with the existing and prospective new Regional Associations.

With the increase in public subsidy, a heavy responsibility attaches to its administrators to deal with matters on a basis of knowledge. You cannot acquaint yourself with these fields in a few hours or a few days; many of them require a lifelong study. The advantage of committees of enquiry is that even if their members do not possess lifelong experience on all aspects, they can call into counsel or evidence the people who do, and can use their own skill in selection. I believe that committees of enquiry of this kind will be necessary in a number of areas of artistic activity, but we are always held back by the recognition that the greater part of the work that needs to be done by and for this Council is voluntarily undertaken by people already very busily engaged in other spheres. Nor can this be helped. The 'volunteers' are an indispensable and invaluable part of the structure of English social life, particularly so where the development of the arts is concerned, so that we must willingly accept the minor disadvantages of not being able to use them as often or as arduously as we might wish.

Travel is supposed to broaden the mind, and it has furnished me with the following reflections. Recently I had cause to pay a brief (although from my point of view sufficiently prolonged) visit to a 'luxury' island packed with income tax-saving tycoons. The island was regaled with a great many features of gracious living, luxury hotels, casinos, yachts, restaurants and other delights, but it seemed as though an immensely powerful and invisible Philistine hand had carefully throttled any nourishment for the human mind. The only live entertainment I could find was an amateur theatrical production, bravely performed under conditions of hideous adversity, on a stage composed of soap boxes, in sweltering heat slightly aggravated by a solitary fan. Any one of the tycoons could have provided a theatre of the size required by the island, without the naked eye detecting any appreciable fall in his or her bank balance. That he or she did not do so was not meanness, but the sheer and near impossibility of any such project being evolved without some form of public organization to control and canalize it. It left me the more convinced of the Arts Council's essential function, not as the universal provider, but as the centre and focus of activities which might otherwise remain forever unrealized hopes. In contrast, my trip took me on to the more familiar ground of New York, another look at the Lincoln Centre and its immense splendour, and a realization that here was private wealth lavished with care and thought beyond our wildest dreams. But it left me without any sense of envy, because it was clear to me that this pattern of patronage produced magnificent charitable donations which blossomed in the territories irrigated by the pools of vast local wealth, but left arid and barren the areas without such pools. This would not do for our notions of a New Society.

This is no criticism of the United States of America but it does, I think, reflect something of the differences of approach and philosophy that make the Arts Council a necessary institution for this country, and that even made an Arts Council an emergent institution for the United States.

Our activities remain to a very large extent controlled by the funds available to us. Not wholly, because there is assistance which, with imagination and willingness, we can provide that is not restricted to finance; but the money counts to a great extent, and we must hope that, notwithstanding the recurring economic crises which, as some wag remarked, 'had made the wolf at the door a household animal,' a civilized government (of any political colour) will continue to recognize that our function is an indispensable one in a civilized society. We are not a luxury; we do not cater for a small *élite* out of the pockets of a protesting multitude; we supply a commodity which a great many people require and which can make a better life for a great many more, once their interest and appetite have been awakened.

1969

I believe that the last thirty years in this country have demonstrated a profound social change. Within our society there is now a widespread feeling that the provision of drama and music and painting and all culture in its broadest sense is no longer to be regarded as a privilege for a few, but is the democratic right of the entire community. I think that any government – and happily there is no sign of any such government – that attempted to reverse this trend would find very rapidly how strong and deep it ran.

During the year there has been considerable and ever-increasing

Arts Council activity at hand. First and foremost we had to deal with the investigation of the Estimates Committee. That Britain is no longer 'the country without music' (or any of the other arts for that matter) is largely due to the patient work of the Arts Council over the past twenty years or so in supporting and encouraging performing, and to a lesser extent, creative artists. It must surely therefore appear a more than usually odd paradox that the nation spent as much in 1965–66 on military bands as was given to the Arts Council, even after the substantial increases in grant. These increases were absolutely and proportionately considerable, but it is clear that there is still a long way to go, even if the road has an end.

The Report has not merely vindicated the exertions of twenty-one years – a mere five so far as I personally am concerned – but has, I believe, achieved a healthy public purpose in dispelling, through the eyes and mouth of a completely objective and impartial body, a number of the legends and myths with which we are beset.

First, it is immensely satisfactory to find that, although the ambit of the Committee's inquiries extended to a great many Arts Council subsidized organizations (the Committee were prepared to receive evidence from anybody, however disgruntled – the gruntled rarely give evidence), not a single instance was brought to their notice, or suggested, of extravagance or wastage by Arts Council customers. And there was not a vestige of a suggestion – as indeed we should hope would be the case – of anything but the most proper and scrupulous use of the funds which we so widely disburse into so many quarters.

It is an immense tribute to the artistic beneficiaries of this country that an investigation of this kind should conclude with a totally negative result on these scores, and it would be wrong if we did not react to these conclusions with a faint suggestion of pride and even of trumpet-blowing.

But, of course, the thrift and probity of financial administration, necessary as they are, do not vindicate the ultimate use of the money. What was no less satisfactory was the emphatic conclusion arrived at by the Committee that what we were doing needed to be done, and, what is more, that the sums of money we were administering were inadequate, and should be augmented on a scale which we ourselves had never had the temerity to suggest. But we shall, now.

1970

The year under review had ended before the Election – in which the support of the Arts was certainly not the determining issue – had with scant ceremony whisked away our beloved first Minister of the Arts. I have paid tribute to her elsewhere and no one could have paid more generous tribute to her than her successor, Viscount Eccles, whose willingness to speak well of the work done before his advent sets a new and most welcome precedent in political generosity.

He has a job of fascinating interest and challenging importance. At the Arts Council we shall contract astigmatism by keeping our eyes fixed on him with steady and unwavering hope. He is a cultivated man who has established his personal love for the arts, and our first encounters with him have been stimulating. Since we believe that what we are doing is good and necessary, it is gratifying to find him of the same belief. And we are much sustained by the knowledge that his principal colleague has installed a musical instrument which cannot be operated mechanically. It should encourage the increasing minority clinging desperately to alternatives to television as the only home entertainment.

But the reference to television must remind us of what it is all about. It is about our conviction that the artist's message is a unique commentary on human affairs which, read with understanding, enriches the lives of the readers. We do not succumb to the error that this message can be understood without effort and study. It may be a mass message but it is not a message to a mass. It speaks to everyone as an individual.

Inevitably a change of government, involving more than anything a change of social and political philosophy, must cause questioning about State support for any activity. We have frequently repudiated the extremists who regard the State's as the only appropriate purse to finance artistic projects. It is inconceivable that such a notion should be acceptable in a free society.

But we are unrepentant in our belief that whatever the political faith of the government administering us, there is an area of artistic activity that must wither and die without help from the public purse. The test of eligibility for support is easier to sense than to define, but in broad terms the beneficiary objective must have merit or promise of merit, appeal or prospect of appeal, and must satisfy a discriminating need. The importance of an audience response is a variable factor. If it is a commodity which depends for its survival on the response of an audience – such as a theatre or a concert hall – it is a nonsense to subsidize an activity that produces no such reaction. But it is equally wrong to measure its value solely in audience terms. Hence if a repertory theatre which performs a range of relatively popular plays fails to draw an adequate audience, it is plain that it should be re-sited or change its policy, or even, as the final decision, be closed. But if subsidy is for a poet, his recognition by a single perceptive mind can amply justify support to maintain an activity which can rarely find an adequate public.

The fallacy is to believe that artistic activities, at present supported by us and other local or charitable bodies, could in fact be transferred to commercial managements. The fate of the London theatre has demonstrated that, except in the rarest instances, we have contrived an economic world where it is a simple untruth that worthwhile activities must necessarily succeed. The sad fact is that the best of newspapers, the best of books, and the best of magazines have no economic security in a society whose values are totally insecure. No small repertory theatre need reproach itself that its box office receipts cannot maintain the performances even if it is playing to near-capacity, when we realize that newspapers with circulations in the region of two million readers cannot, in the 'Alice in Wonderland' world in which we live, make a sufficient profit to safeguard their survival. We do not believe that these simple economic propositions need reinforcing in the decision-making quarters of any government. The Arts Council received encouragement from each successive government in turn and will, we are confident, continue to receive it so long as the attainment of a more civilized society remains the ultimate objective of all political exertions.

But generalities about the virtuous and beneficent nature of our activities are of little value unless they are supported by knowledge and care and thought in our administration. Each year that passes makes me the more convinced that we are still faltering towards answers; that increasing experience and study will, in the future, effect radical changes in our practices and even our precepts. But we cannot be accused of a refusal to learn. In the year that we cover we published a further two Reports on aspects of Arts Council life – Opera and Ballet. Both demonstrated the time and effort generously volunteered by busy people to enable their compilation. Both have already been of great use and will be of continuing use as blueprints in our future planning.

I would wish that there might be a million Arts Councils in this country – so that there might be a million men who enjoy the benefits of training as their Chairmen. There is no more liberal education available in the whole wide world. In six years of enthralling office I have – unlike the Bourbons – learnt more and forgotten more than in any period of my life. A Chairman of the Arts Council finds that every preconception in relation to the administration of the Arts is either mistaken or at least calls for massive qualification. If the wicked can ever hope for leisure, I shall hope one day to write at greater length on this theme. As it is I am satisfied that a sanhedrim of Arts Council Chairmen would solve every human problem – except the artistic ones – with effortless ease. We shall expect the summons shortly after the publication of this report. For who can have the experience in travel that is available to a Chairman of the Arts Council? In the last two years I have recorded something of my adventures. This year I was off again to worlds totally new to me and indeed totally new. I attended an Arts Council Conference in New Zealand, where for many days passionate zealots read papers to each other about how best to disperse a tiny grant in a tiny country. Every one of the problems we have encountered and are still encountering here. Should the money be spent on one major artistic institution, designed to set standards, to be followed up by expansion elsewhere when (the same hope is entertained the world over) increasing enlightenment in government produces increases resources? Or should it from the outset be spent in tiny packets throughout the territory? The regionalists see little prospect of frequent visits to the metropolitan centres and urged wide-scale distribution. The urban centres and a few of the more far-sighted urged that at the outset at least one or two important artistic institutions should be set up. These views could not be reconciled, but they could be argued out in splendid rhetoric, and they were. For the delegates at that conference, during the days that it occupied, there was nothing else going on in the universe. One met again with pleasure the fervour of real enthusiasts who believe in their cause.

I met the same thing again in Australia but of course on a larger scale. Sydney is a great urban centre – with a population of three million people. It has artistic ambitions on an impressive scale. The story of its Opera House has many very creditable elements. Heaven knows when it will be completed or how much it will have cost, but I have a feeling that when it is completed its cost will be repaid by the influence it will exercise. Future generations will, I believe, give the thanks to the city fathers who have decided to build it that are not immediately forthcoming from their present ancestors.

My visits reinforced the moral that the spread of the arts can be no faster than the speed at which an artistic public can become educated. But it cannot become educated unless the Arts Councils of Australia and New Zealand and other similar organizations, now mushrooming all over the world, are there to make available the world's resources of music, painting, literature and drama. And these remote places continue to demonstrate the invincible determination of a few people to make a better world, undeterred by the fact that many of their fellow countrymen could not be dragged to a cultural activity by a team of wild kangaroos. They plod on with sense and discretion to ensure that the next generation should not be similarly deprived. It is the next generation and the generations to come upon whom we must set our eyes.

3. The Arts in Britain

Additional sums of money have been voted to us, very generously, by a Government which has shown a most progressive and liberal attitude to the arts. But the fact remains that those sums of money are not yet adequate. I do not belong to the school which says that we need vast fortunes for the arts. We probably could not today use a budget of three times what we have, because we are not yet geared to administer it. But I hope that, if I may have the good fortune to continue my term of office, by the time that period has elapsed we shall have a budget of some such order and shall be geared to administer it. But the arts do not call for such sums of money.

We are not here to administer and control the artistic life and effort and output of the country. It would be a horrible thing if any bureaucratic organization had that function, and I wish to say, as publicly as possible, that if the day comes when an author has to turn to the Arts Council before he can write a book, or a dramatist before he can write a play, or a manager before he can present it, I should not wish to be administering the affairs of that body.

It remains very much my hope that the greater part of the artistic effort and incentive of this country will arise from spontaneous inspiration without the slightest reference to us. We are an auxiliary body, and we shall remain an auxiliary body. We are not here to control artistic output; we are not here to regulate what artists are doing; we are not here to promote artistic activity all over the country.

It is not our job to say that we suspect that there is a relapse by some children who we have indoctrinated with Bartok for the last six weeks and are suspected now of possessing Beatle records, and that we are landing by parachute parts of orchestral symphonies to redress that situation. This is not what we are there for, and I hope that we shall never undertake any such duty.

Our job is to deal with applications when they come to us from people who have originated them on the spot. It is not our job to send pre-packaged commodities, pre-packaged cultural parcels from the metropolis to other parts of the country. Nothing will arouse greater resentment than that we should probe about all over the place telling parts of the country that they are insufficiently cultured and that they need some particular cultural activity. What we must do when we get cries for assistance when a local authority comes to us – and almost all we do in these matters today is in the most friendly partnership and association with the local authorities – is to give them all the help we can, and to decide how to apportion the financial cost. Here we have many an argument with them. May I say that it is a friendly argument, but it is a sensible one. They have a means of providing money from a budget which is not as rigorously controlled as our own, and naturally we are anxious, and sometimes adamant, that it should come from their purse and not ours.

I have said before, and I say again now, that I do not think the question of local option in relation to financing artistic areas in this country is especially a wise one. I should like to see a mandatory obligation placed on local authorities, giving them not merely a discretion but an actual duty to spend a specific sum of money. This is perhaps a controversial point, but I would invite the Government at some time to consider whether it should not be investigated. It places local authorities in a great difficulty. They have an election coming. They do not know, and they cannot assess, how many people are 'pro-art' or 'anti-art'. Factors that have little or nothing to do with the matter are therefore introduced into a question that ought to be totally unpolitical. It is for that reason that I think local authorities should be relieved of the burden of having to make decisions which will have electoral consequences.

Here perhaps I ought to say a word about the constitution of the Arts Council. Our authority derives from the Charter granted to us, a new Charter granted at the beginning of this year. That is the document to which we turn. We are subject to no governmental control; we would not respond to governmental control, and it is desperately important that we should make a selection of members of the Council that manifests this matter beyond any peradventure. I hope that we have done this.

Without any invidious naming of persons, I would draw attention to my own participation in this since the Council was appointed. The appointments are, of course, made by the Minister. They are made on recommendation and after discussions with the Sovereign. Since my appointment as Chairman of the Arts Council there have been four new members. The first of them was Sir Edward Boyle; the second was Lord Harewood; the third was Sir Joseph Lockwood, the head of the great electronic organization; and the fourth was Mr. Angus Wilson, the novelist. It is a fact that, of every member of the Council, the only one whose political views I know is Sir Edward Boyle, for the obvious reason that I could not fail to know. I have never heard the question of politics being discussed in any Arts Council matter. I could not conceive how it would arise. I think this is a reassurance that one cannot stress too often.

I believe it is very important indeed that we should regionalize to the extent that we depute a large measure of our functions and responsibility to associations like the North East Association for the Arts. I hope they will take various forms, and the reason is this. This is an experimental matter, the organization of which has yet to be determined. I think it will be a very good thing if in the different areas they take a different shape and we can elect by experience, empirically, the one which is best suited to serve the purposes of the particular area and which perhaps can serve as a model and prototype for other areas. The North East Association for the Arts is a good body; it is an amalgam of our own personnel, our own grants, of local authorities, of industry, and with some private assistance. It works to bring all the elements with a desire to subsidize a system to promote the arts into a single consortium. It is working well, but I think it might well take other shapes in other places. This is an activity which we want to promote on the basis that it is extremely important that we should not allow everything to happen in London.

Here I will say a word on this evergreen question of the conflicts between the claims of London and those of the regions. London is a capital city; it must have the furnishings of a capital city. A civilized country must have a great and good quality opera house. It should have a fine national theatre, fine concert halls. These I would not really regard as counting towards the total sum at all, because they are available to everyone, and to talk as if England was a country where it was necessary to travel for seven days on a camel in order to reach London is, I think, a rather absurd presentation of the picture.

But the fact remains that it is in the regions that actual inspiration and growth arise. Leaving aside the question of the furnishings of a great capital city, I think the most important work that we can do today is to promote regional artistic activity. We shall not find in London a sufficient coherence of population to be able to do that sort of thing. In London you promote and support individual artistic effort. In the regions there is a community effort which can be supported and can be brought to a rich fulfilment and blossoming. This is something which we have to bear very prominently in mind. The expenditure on the regions, leaving aside the great centres, leaving aside the National Theatre, the Opera House, and so forth, has now outpaced and exceeded the expenditure one finds in London. I do not think the regions have any legitimate cause for complaint at all.

I am unrepentant in saying that my own personal view is that it would be quite wrong to erect a second national opera house in London before there was a vestige of an opera house in Manchester, or in Edinburgh or in any other part of England. We made a considered decision, and I believe it to be right. That it has caused regret to someone who had an alternative great plan and conception must be a cause of regret to us all, but the fact remains that it was indeed the right thing to do.

Another matter which Lord Cottesloe raised, and one of primary importance, was the question of quality. He expressed a concern, and a legitimate concern, that as our activities grew wider, as we spread the money more widely, there might be the possibility of a diminution in the quality and, in the end, the inferior article would destroy the taste for the thing altogether. He thought we might, by providing too much, defeat the very objective we were seeking. I think that this is a real risk, but not as real a risk as Lord Cottesloe believes, because there is a difference in our philosophy, if I may be permitted to say so. I do not regard it as the function of the Arts Council to judge the quality of every performance in every part of the country. This I regard as the function of the organizations to which we give the money.

I think it of the greatest importance that we should not seek to establish from St James's Square a censorship over all art. All the organizations which receive money from us should know that they are autonomous and are free to do what they like with it, subject to the qualification that there is proper accounting and that, in the end, there is sufficient public service benefit – sufficient value to the public for the expenditure of that money.

This is a very difficult question; it is a matter of degree. If you have a poet, he may be the most obscure poet and he may attract only a few hundred people to his readership, but he may be a man who is well worthy of support, and it would be wrong for a civilized country not to support him. If you have an opera company, a totally different consideration arises. It would be wrong to continue to subsidize an opera company which was producing operas that played to empty houses night after night. This is the sort of consideration that weighs with us. It has to be considered individually in respect of each application. There are no rules that can be laid down, no criteria that can be applied, except the criterion of common sense. This is what we try to do, in a fallible way. What we have to seek to avoid desperately is the notion that within St James's Square we have the best answer as to what the artistic values are: that we know what is good art and other people do not. Obviously we have experts; we can provide sound judgments; but, if we look at the matter historically, how many generations have succeeded in identifying all their geniuses in their own time? What a piece of arrogance and folly it would be on our part to believe that we possess this faculty, when nobody else has possessed it previously!

Plainly, we must take the widest possible spread to ensure that we avoid, not the danger that we may waste money on a non-genius – this, where we are spending one-hundredth part of the expenditure on scientific discoveries, seems to me a trifle – but the danger that we may not subsidize the genius. That is the danger we must seek to avoid. Obviously, we must not waste money on absurdities – and a lot is said and written about the marginal absurdities of the arts. We are told about artistic works which nobody can understand; we are told about concrete poetry, and all the things the man in the street is supposed to have no use or value for. It is within this atmosphere of latitude towards experiment, the attitude of accepting new and novel ideas, even if they are personally alien to us, that the artist can thrive and live. It is therefore quite right that a small portion of our money should be spent on what appears to some people to be manifest absurdities. I make no apology for this at all. If we were spending great sums of money on these absurdities there would be legitimate cause for complaint, but it is bound to happen that over the edge there will seep a little money to things which may seem extravagant, too *avant garde*, too 'with it'. This must be the price you pay if you want to win the confidence of artists.

This brings me to artists. An enormously important part of our job is to endeavour to improve the status of the artist. We shall not make artists with money. Nothing we on the Arts Council do will produce a couple of lines; with any amount of money, we shall not produce a sonnet, or even a couplet. No artistic production comes because of the money we have available. What we can do is to ensure that the artist lives in tolerable conditions and is reasonably free from the threat and the sting of poverty, from the fear that, through following an artistic avocation, he will have to go without food and will be unable to educate his children. We ought to be thoroughly ashamed of the situation which prevails in this country at the moment in regard to the rewards to authors. It is not due to anybody or anything: it has just developed.

It is desperately important that we on the Arts Council should promote means of improving those conditions. One thing we have done is to seek to promote certain legislative changes which may be of assistance. One small success we had – and I should like to thank the Government for it – was in procuring in the Budget a minor amelioration of the condition of authors who sell their copyrights. This was an excellent instance of teamwork in the Arts Council. We drafted the Amendment, and Sir Edward Boyle tabled it and moved it in another place last year. It was received sympathetically by the Financial Secretary. Later in the year, before the recent Budget, we wrote and asked, 'What are you going to do about it? We should like some manifestation of action.' He received a small deputation, consisting of Sir Edward Boyle, members of the Society of Authors and myself, and we discussed the matter at length. He has not given us what we wanted, but we have got something which is of real value and will be of assistance to the author, and particularly the retired author.

The author in later life who wants to sell a copyright, who finds perhaps that he is no longer writing, will be able to spread over a number of years the money that he receives. To a large extent he will in doing so retrieve a substantial part of the purchase price. One does not wish over-much to promote the sale of copyrights – it is not a good thing – but it is far better to have that situation than the rather humiliating situation now prevailing, when many distinguished authors have to sell their manuscripts to American universities as the only means of remaining alive. This is something that will specially touch the heart chords of the noble Lord, Lord Cottesloe, because he was talking about the export of works of art. This is something which is far more general, far more prevalent and which could far more easily be stopped. It is very important that we should take steps to try to promote and advance the incomes and earnings of authors and other artists.

One way by which we hope to do it, on which we have been working very hard, is to promote a public lending right. This is a controversial question. I have no doubt at all in my own mind that common justice demands that when a book is borrowed from a library 500 or 1,000 times the author should receive some reward. It seems to me completely inexcusable, as a matter of equity, that an author should receive only one payment when a book is read by hundreds if not thousands of people. It is a difficult question, and when one tries to promote legislation one is invariably met with the argument that it is impossible to produce legislation that does not involve anomalies; that there will be inequities and injustices whatever is done. This seems to me to be an argument entirely without merit. It is suggested that because we cannot achieve, as I am sure we cannot, total justice, we should be satisfied with total injustice. I hope that before long someone will be presenting in your Lordships' House a measure for the amelioration of this situation. I know – and I am pleased to be able to say it – that this view, in principle, has the good will and sympathy of the Government. They are waiting to see what sort of measure can be introduced and whether it will be an effective and workable one. This is something which we are working on in the Arts

Council, and it is another of the things which we are doing in a new development of an administrative character.

We are also investigating the possibilities of expanding the value of the money we spend, by a greater use of television and radio. One of the things which struck many of us as an anomaly was that thousands, if not hundreds of thousands, of pounds would be spent on great operatic performances and great theatrical performances, which could of necessity be shown only to small audiences. The obvious solution is to see whether those performances can be put on television, whether there is any prospect of showing them to multiple audiences all over the country, so getting real money and real value for the expenditure. We have a committee, chaired by Sir Edward Boyle, which is at this moment investigating this question. It is a slow process: it will involve negotiations with the BBC and ITV companies, but in the end, if we can produce something along these lines, I think that there will be a very fruitful result.

Our major emphasis is on cultivating new audiences for the arts. The question of improving the standard and quality of those institutions which are still there is of great importance, but it is not our paramount consideration. Frankly, if we were concerned only with the question of whether we could have a better production of *Traviata* tonight at Covent Garden than we had last year, my own interest in the matter would not be so keen. I do not deny the importance of these matters, but I am concerned with something which I think is more fundamental.

I believe that there is a crucial state in the country at this moment. I believe that young people lack values, lack certainties, lack guidance; that they need something to turn to; and need it more desperately than they have needed it at any time in our history – certainly at any time which I can recollect. I do not say that the arts will furnish a total solution, but I believe that the arts will furnish some solution. I believe that once young people are captured for the arts they are redeemed from many of the dangers which confront them at the moment and which have been occupying the attention of the Government in a completely unprofitable and destructive fashion. I believe that here we have constructive work to do which can be of inestimable value. So long as we do not over-assess our importance, so long as we keep a sense of balance, and so long as we realize that it is not for us to adjudicate on all artistic questions, and that everyone's viewpoint must be taken into consideration, then I think there is much we can do that is of value.

(Speech in the House of Lords, April 19, 1967)

4. Jennie Lee: Minister

No true democrat can wholly deplore a change of government. It indicates that the system works and that it will go on working. Nor, ordinarily, need one shed many tears for unseated politicians, a fraternity of robust qualities including the more rugged attributes of a sorbo ball – harder hit, higher bounce. But once in an eon there is universal and unpolitical regret at the departure of a distinguished public figure.

The Arts Council is, and always has been, in position and sentiment, an apolitical body. It has drawn its strength and support from every government in power during its short existence of just over a quarter of a century. It is nevertheless proper that, as it extends welcome to Lord Eccles, it should say a word of appreciation to its very first Minister with duties exclusively devoted to the arts.

I have rarely met such unanimity of regret expressed in so widespread a circle as at the end of Jennie Lee's House of Commons career. But she will not encourage any elegiac note. Miss Lee is not one to promote wakes in her lifetime. When I telephoned her on Friday last – faintly apprehensive about her mood – the same clear, strong voice replied with the same indomitable spirit. She was, she said, more than half-pleased that she had left her seat. If the Government were defeated she had no real wish to function again in the Commons in opposition, and, of course, she was right. For one of the amazing achievements of this remarkable woman has been to take the area of her parliamentary activity almost entirely out of politics.

Despite the occasional screeches of those who regard it as indecent that any public activity should have a non-political flavour, she had contrived a situation probably unequalled in living memory. If one examines the *Hansards* of the last Government it is almost impossible to find a really discordant note relating to her activities or the expression of a contrary viewpoint that has any political flavour, and to the credit of her political opponents, they responded in precisely the same spirit. There was a universal recognition enhanced by her policy and her own attitudes, that public sponsorship of the arts – on a scale, although still modest, exceeding anything that had previously been practised by any previous government – was only respectable if it was freed from political direction or control. This was a doctrine she enunciated firmly and clearly and maintained to the end of her regime. Previously it had been implicit – now it was expressed. It has done more good for public sponsorship of the arts, exposed more clearly the fallacies of any other policy and the shortcomings of other countries in this respect than any other single public attitude. Moreover, she accepted – not always without legitimate misgivings – the corollary of this policy; that those upon whom the bounty was carefully bestowed must have as much freedom of action as can be contrived, and that political control must not accompany any subsidy.

In a short appreciation it is not possible to dwell in detail with the major activities of the Lee era. Mistakes there were; uncertainties there were, but they did not derive from vacillation of policy or feebleness of purpose. It is not right for me to attempt an assessment of their success or their durability. But the one view – unalterably held by the Arts Council – is that we have had a Minister of rare quality. Jennie Lee is not a great intellectual and she claimed no profound knowledge of the arts. But she secured the confidence of artists, great and small, talented and less talented. They instinctively felt the profundity of her belief that the artist was the most important member of the community; of her other belief that the first essential of a civilized country was to promote the interests of the artists and to make art in every sense available to the greatest number.

She met, of course, the élitist argument that art was decreed by the Almighty for the few; and that an increasing size of audience would necessarily imperil the quality. She treated this as the poppycock it was; and she is a woman who speaks her mind firmly. But for all that, she made no enemies and countless friends, and she was an inspiration for youth who for her could do little wrong.

There is, happily, no need to speak of her in the past tense. There is much that still remains for her to do. To many she is known as the overlord Minister of the Arts Council, but there was much more to her work. Almost single-handed she has brought into being the University of the Air, an experiment which has aroused interest throughout the educational world. In her regime the National Theatre at long last, too, came to be built. She has contrived the establishment of a National Film School. She saved the Tate Gallery from a demented (but unavoidable) amputation by persuading the Government to make additional land available for sensible expansion. She gave support and wise counsel to the problems of the British Museum. She has been a friend to art galleries throughout the country and done everything within her power to promote important purchases. She was tireless in visiting artistic activities large and small throughout the country. Her handsome face and winning accents became known everywhere, but her shopping list – as she called her unfulfilled programme – was endless except in the sight of eternity. Above all, I would pay tribute to a rare and generous gift of friendship of which I, and countless others, have been grateful beneficiaries.

(Evening Standard, June 25, 1970)

5. Public Lending Right and Regional Subsidy

The artist is of course the most important man in any civilized society. He is the man who counts for most and who brings the greatest pleasure, to whom we owe the greatest debt of gratitude. But what we have to realize – and I think I said this the last time we had a debate – is that no amount of money, no amount of cosseting, no amount of legislation on our part, is going to produce art, good or bad. Artists are not produced by our exertions. Artists can be encouraged by our exertions, and the point that I think needs to be made, and needs to be made constantly, is that while we shall not produce artists by making money available, while we shall not produce artists by making living conditions better for them, we owe it to artists and we owe it to ourselves, as a civilized community, to see that the working conditions of artists are tolerable and that they do not live in penury and in circumstances of difficulty.

Hence I am quite unrepentant at coming back to this question of what is called the 'public lending right'. The point was raised by the noble Viscount, Lord Norwich, and I am sure it will be raised by other speakers. If I may say so, the noble Lord, Lord Kennet, dealt with it with masterly diplomacy, but I do not believe that it presents any of the difficulties that he raised. It seems to me that there is an arguable case in relation to it. Here is the simple case of one man misusing another man's intellectual property. When you have a book you buy that book for your own use. No canon of natural justice should entitle you to let it out to 150 different people and make no payment of any kind to the man who had originally written the book. I should require a lot of persuading that this was a right and a just thing to do and that in a civilized society we cannot find a means of rectifying that simple injustice.

We could rectify it by means of a very small amendment to our copyright law. That would leave the position in which nobody would be entitled to do this, and the libraries would have to put the position right by making their own terms with the owners of the books as the situation arose. There are a dozen ways in which the position could be rectified. The Arts Council have produced a scheme. I think it is quite a good scheme. It has its anomalies, it has its difficulties, it has its obvious injustices; but I have said on several occasions, and I say again, that it cannot be a reason for refusing to alter a situation of total injustice that one cannot effect total justice. I am sure it must be right to find some means of putting this scheme into operation.

There is one misconception that I think gives rise to a lot of the trouble, and that is the notion of the sanctity of the free library. I should be the last person to suggest that that notion should in any sense be compromised, but I think there is a misconception. A 'free library' means a library which is free to the subscriber; it does not mean a library which is free of cost to the community. To use a library necessarily involves costs on a number of scores: it is impossible to run a library without charges for the repair of the building, the cost of the staff, the purchase of the books and a multitude of other items. This is only one item that should be added to these others which, for some reason, it has been decided should be charged to the unfortunate authors, the section of the community that can least afford it.

I would make a plea to the Government that although this is a matter of money, that although it is a matter of a couple of million pounds, it is an act of justice that is long overdue. We of the Arts Council would very much welcome some sign that, even if it is not to be done today, at least the Government have it in mind for introduction as soon as the economic situation makes it a possibility. The authors' recent resentment at the situation was expressed in what I felt was a most unjustifiable attack on the Minister – a very great Minister, if I may venture to say so, and the last person in the world who should have been subjected to that sort of attack. One can understand their recent resentment, because when people are resentful they are not particularly cautious in their choice of words or their choice of targets; but it is singularly ironic that they should have chosen a Minister who has pledged such full and vigorous support to the arts on all fronts, and to this scheme in particular. I would urge the Government to consider this matter as sympathetically as possible.

May I turn to another subject which I think is of very considerable consequence, another recent rumpus between ourselves and the regions. I do not think that this is a rumpus (if I may use that inelegant word in this Chamber) that has operated throughout the country. I think it is a rather localized rumpus, but it is one that needs to be touched on, and I think if I may say so that the noble Lord, Lord Kennet, dealt with it in absolutely impeccable fashion. I should like to endorse his words, because it would be most unfortunate if an impression got around that there was some sort of competition between London and the regions as to the distribution of the artistic benefits that are available. There is no competition. There is, again, a great misconception, and it arises from the fact that certain people seem to believe that we are able to start from scratch. But of course we are not. It must be remembered that the Arts Council have been working for more than the two or three years of which we are taking notice at this moment: the Council have been working tirelessly and effectively for many years. Enormous credit attaches to my predecessors, and particularly to the dedicated staffs who have been working right up to now. I do not think anyone could praise the staffs too highly for the work they do and the devotion they show, for the care and attention they give, and for their utter disregard of time where the interests of the job are concerned.

But, my Lords, one has to bear in mind that we inherited an existing situation: we did not decide to establish an opera house in London. I am very glad that whoever did decide it did so. We now have a splendid and memorable opera house in London – in fact we have two splendid opera houses in London, and it is quite right that we should have them. But these were existing established institutions. Once there, they had to be paid for. One could not shut them down in order to enter into some academic distribution of the money on an arithmetical basis *per capita* throughout the country. It would not make sense to send to everybody in England a 2s 6d postal order and say: 'We have shut down every artistic institution in all parts of the country but this may be used by you exclusively for artistic purposes. Here is a list of Penguin books of an artistic nature for which the voucher may be changed.' In a sense that is the logic of the regional argument, if carried to its conclusions.

What we must certainly do is to give priority to our great artistic institutions, because they fertilize everything; they set the standards for everything. If you have a first-class opera house of international standard, if you have a great national theatre in which we can all take pride, if you have a second great national theatre, of the type which exists at Stratford and is also to be found in London, if you have great orchestras of the kind we have now succeeded in establishing, then you have standards by which artistic activity can grow and flourish all over the country. But what you cannot do is to discuss this matter in simple arithmetical terms; that everyone in Wales ought to have 3s 2d, and everyone in Cullompton ought to have 1s 9d.

I am sure there are areas that are at present painfully deprived because there are no artistic activities of any kind, and the most painfully deprived areas of all are to be found in London. I would invite your Lordships to take a drive with me to the suburbs of London and see what artistic activities you can find in mile after mile. The notion that London is well served, to the detriment of the regions, is great nonsense. London is much worse served, outside the centre, than many of the regional areas. What we have decided is that, as a matter of simple justice, expenditure in London must pretty well cease, and we must concentrate on spending the money for the benefit of people who are too far removed to have somewhere within their vicinity to find the artistic activities which we regard as valuable and worth while.

The whole problem is simply one of money. The noble Lord, Lord Nugent, was absolutely right when he said that if we were to spend all the money that we could spend, if we were to present a budget of the size that we could quite easily compose, it would be so formidable as to daunt a great section of the population. Hence we have to engage in this matter with a great deal of sense, a great deal of reserve, and a great deal of circumspection and discretion. You cannot make demands on people for enormous sums of money simply because it would be desirable to have half a dozen opera houses established in various parts of the country. You must proceed by degrees. You must acclimatize people to the notion that this is an expenditure which is part of the ordinary expenditure of civilized life and is part of the educative process.

On this point I would take exception to an article that I read last Sunday, in a newspaper that ought to know better, dealing with the question of subsidizing the arts. That particular newspaper raised the question of how the money was to be found, and it again used this popular phrase about 'providing arts for a small *élite*'. But this is by no means the case. We have recently engaged a statistician, and between us we have done a little work. We have never arrived at a satisfactory conclusion, because there is a highly conjectural element in the arithmetic concerned. But if you take into consideration the audiences that attend concerts by all the nine symphony orchestras that we subsidize in England, the audiences that attend the sixty-odd repertory theatres we subsidize, the audiences that go to the Opera House (which I believe holds 2,300) each evening, eight performances a week; and if you take into consideration the audiences that go to the National Theatre and to the Coliseum (holding 2,700 people), you will, I think, find that, far from there being a small *élite*, there are many millions of people who have a direct interest in, and who benefit from, the activities of the Arts Council. So it is great nonsense to regard this matter as one that affects only a small *élite* and that the mass of the population should show resentment because money is spent in this fashion. We are dealing here with the interests of an ever-increasing minority, and I believe that minority to be capable of an even greater increase.

One of my favourite analogies is to relate to the time, 150 years ago, when a great many people believed that the percentage of literacy in our population had been predetermined by the Almighty – it was, I believe, ten per cent. Happily, there were dedicated people, enlightened people, who did not accept these statistics and who were firmly convinced that if education were made available that statistic could be altered for the better. Time has shown how right they were. Time will show how right we are in believing that the numbers of people who can enjoy the fruits of art, the number of people who can enjoy reading good literature, enjoy seeing great plays, enjoy hearing fine music, is not as bounded as we think it is. It may be that this enjoyment will not extend to the entire population; it may be that there will always be people who will prefer other activities to this – and why not? Good luck to them!

But, my Lords, I am firmly convinced that, with a proper education and a proper expenditure of effort, the number can be increased beyond our dreams at this moment of time. That is why I think the present Government have been so wise and so provident in making the provision they have made. That is why, if I may say so, I shall not lose the opportunity of urging upon this Government that they should continue with this splendid work. I know of no work that they can better do than this. I know of no expenditure in relation to the small sums involved that is more valuable or better spent. May I end by taking the opportunity of saying how grateful I personally am to the Government for what has been done; how well I believe this money to have been used, and how much I hope they will continue with that work and that we shall have bigger and better opportunities of using such money in the future.

(Speech in the House of Lords, February 26, 1969)

6. The Book and the Patron

When I was invited to write this piece I was a little puzzled about its general scheme – the future of books. To me books have no special future differing from their present, and the situation is not altered by possibilities of publication in different buildings, with different prints; in larger or smaller editions, on microfilm, or whatever other form the unnecessary meddlings of technology may bring. But it seemed that my sanguine view was not shared by everyone. There was, I was told, a distinct school of young opinion that the book is a 'dead institution'. It would sully the scholarly pages of the TLS to reproduce my comment. To reject the book is to reject the mind. The human race can no more abandon it than it can abandon the drinking of water. The proposition is aired by the illiterates who, up till now, have not read books, but find that the omission can now be supported by arguments of specious respectability. They do not speak for the young or the middle-aged or any other group of humans; they speak only for the apes. Thus, this article postulates that the reading habit will continue and that book buying will continue.

The human practice which over the ages has brought more contentment of mind and more happiness is not, I like to believe, in any danger. And if I am wrong and the best of human life, as we know it, is in danger, it will not be saved by enunciating philosophical dogmas, but by continuing to produce better and better books without being distracted by sillier and sillier arguments. And if it is also true, as I believe, that humanity owes more to the book than to anything else in the world, then our treatment of authors would be a signal reproach of all humanity.

In this article I am happily not concerned with all humanity, but only with this country, and, while it does not seem that authors are worse treated here than elsewhere, and that in some respects they may get slightly better treatment, we certainly cannot overclaim credit. One of the least impressive liberties is the liberty to starve. This particular liberty is freely accorded to authors. Otherwise the rewards they receive are pathetic, and even more pathetic is the absence of any real concern about their economic position and the immense difficulty of fomenting such a concern even in people whose love of literature is undoubted. Hence the question of subsidy and support is a real and important one deserving of occasional public scrutiny.

Of recent years, some research has been done about the money value of book writing to authors. It demonstrates, except in the rare instances when a book becomes a best-seller or is written by an author who is himself a best-seller, that no one would become an author for the money. It is difficult to think of any occupation that does not give a higher average wage to its practitioner than authorship. The figures bandied about during industrial disputes would be mouth-watering to many a distinguished writer. How much good writing is lost because the author cannot afford to remain a writer must be speculative. Hopefully we believe that authors as a community are kinder to their public than their public deserves. They continue to write despite every discouragement, but it would be an optimistic quietening of our social conscience to accept that some writing and perhaps even great writing is not being lost to the world because of the author's poverty, and the need to provide himself with food, clothing and a roof. It is on this score that the question of patronage (an unpleasant word), either public or private, arises. There is no sphere of creative activity where it creates greater difficulties than in authorship. It is not an accident that the Arts Council's Literature Panel was the last to be established; still deploys only a minute fragment of our entire grant; and is still in an early chrysalis stage of development.

We have comforted ourselves by the thought – in which there is much truth – that authorship is well supported by a strong publishing industry aware of its social responsibilities and with a tradition for maintaining penniless authors until they achieve recognition. There is a good deal of truth in this belief, but, like all generalizations, it has important exceptions. Many authors of quality have lived out a life in penury. Many authors of quality have met constant rejection from publishers. Today this latter is a decreasing possibility. The willingness of publishers seemingly to publish anything might mean that, as the greater includes the less, the vast undiscriminating bulk will inevitably include works of quality, but there is a risk that lack of discrimination may well be a meter which responds to rubbish and rejects excellence. We shall not know for a very long time how many authors are being lost to this present generation because of lack of recognition, and indeed, we may never know at all. We have, of course, publishers of keen literary discrimination, men of letters well able to identify talent, but they are not of such numbers that we can be sure that talent will necessarily find them, or, in the vast bulk of manuscripts that have to be read, that sheer exhaustion may not put aside the one of high talent.

Also, the current literary situation from the point of view of authorship has suffered some adverse changes. The literary agent (men like J. B. Pinker) – potent figures in support of a client in whom they had faith – is disappearing from the scene. There are a few very honourable survivors, but the new agent is not unnaturally attracted by the new possibilities. If he can find one client who can sell his film rights for £150,000 or write a television series for some equally astronomical sum, or serialize his account of his escape from the belly of a whale, he naturally prefers to concentrate on these potential gold-mines.

These prospects reduce his interest in the young poet or the young novelist, from whom ten per cent of a few hundred pounds will not, today, pay for the office nibs.

Also the old tradition of the publishers' reader seems to have vanished. Legendary figures like Edward Garnett cannot flourish under the publishing conditions of today. In their day, a very few of such men could influence for the good the prospects of many struggling authors.

It is also unhappily the case that developments claimed as beneficial to the writer – the creation of new media in television, radio and film – may, in fact, be a smaller blessing than is thought. There have been dramatists of genius, like Pinter, emerging from or supported by the world of television, but they need not only to be men of genius, but men of strong character, since television producers arrogate to themselves the right to shape and alter the work. The same is, of course, true of the film – more true. The long-standing Hollywood joke about the non-employment of talented writers who receive huge fees to sit in at story conferences or to watch the mutilation of their books has not altogether ceased to be true. Happily the new director is less and less minded to be restricted even by a book title let alone by its contents, so that the film of today is mercifully individually structured instead of having borrowed from other media. But the effect is that the man who writes for the screen is a writer of extreme specialization, and a different animal from the writer we like to talk about.

Writing of genius represents the unfettered expression of a man's thoughts. It does not represent the expression of a man's thoughts trimmed and tailored for a particular footage of film or minutage of programme, written with an eye on a particular public, and subject to so many other pressures as to make it as much a matter of carpentry as a literary expression. This is no reproach to skilled television and film writers, but it is a recognition that the existence of these media does not necessarily contribute to the treasury of letters, and that the often-heard statement that a writer today enjoys the advantage over his ancestors of employment in television or on the radio or in the cinema is, I believe, a fallacy.

Nor is current journalism as advantageous to the writer as it may previously have been. The magazine for good middlebrow writing (and even for highbrow writing) has largely vanished. In my youth one read Conan Doyle and Somerset Maugham and Stacey Aumonier and H. G. Wells and a host of other respectable names in nice glossy octavo size magazines which even the Chairman of the Arts Council could produce in a railway carriage without shame. All of these have disappeared, as have many of the opportunities for serious journalism. Journalism features today are so self-consciously a part of the circulation war that they have almost no direct relationship with serious writers. Very few editors will publish a feature because of its inherent literary quality. Some of them – not many, alas – might even be able to identify literary quality, but from their point of view it has little point. An advertisement that a feature contains the finest writing of the century might, if it were believed, bring six additional readers for a Sunday Heavy. All these are sad facts which have to be recognized.

In short, the background against which to assess the need for subsidy is discouraging. The immense multiplication of books (not by itself a virtue), the availability of immense sums of money for the written word, the expansion of new fields of activity where writing of some kind is employed – have not been undiluted benefits to the writer and probably, on balance, may have been a positive detriment to literature. Things are not better but worse, because bulk has ousted perception and quality displaced discrimination. Against this background, it is clear to me that artificial support for the writer must be engendered. It is, alas, less clear to others – often in positions of importance. A civilized country ought not to leave its authors to find their own commercial levels of reward.

The discussion must pose the question of how far is money relevant to authorship. History provides no kind of answer.

Certain it is that authorship is not discouraged by the possession of wealth; that (contrary to any current practice) we can safely shower gold nuggets on authors without fear that this will encourage corrupting idleness. It has long been the fact that the practices of drug-addiction and drunkenness which have destroyed many artists of genius are not discouraged by poverty.

The number of great authors from wealthy backgrounds is most encouraging to those who believe that a little wealth is not a bad thing. Tolstoy, perhaps the greatest of all novelists, lived in a world of aristocratic plenty. He might indeed be an argument for outside supervision of the property of authors, since he apparently reduced his thriving estates, under a system incorporating his own lofty morality, to an income so small that his family were in danger of real poverty. It was only when the estates were wrenched back by the indomitable countess that financial equilibrium was restored; but wealth or non-wealth did not interfere with Tolstoy's productivity. Few people could have written more.

Marcel Proust is another instance of a man to whom wealth was irrelevant in artistic terms. He had the money worries of a man of great extravagance, but equally was a man of solid prosperity. His money was useful because it enabled him to pay – to the eternal shame of all French publishers – for the appearance of his early works. It also enabled him to picture a world uniquely suitable for his gifts. Without his money we should not have had his masterpieces. What other masterpieces we might have had, if he had been born the son of a docker at Marseilles, the most ingenious mind cannot speculate.

These and many others support the view that wealth does not distract from writing; not does the advent of prosperity. I heard a successful woman novelist some weeks ago in a radio discussion, airing the view that subsidy for authors would be a bad thing, because it would absolve them from the necessity of taking other jobs, thus reducing the world which they could observe and describe. This is a very arguable proposition. Its relentless logic would have left Dickens in the blacking factory and Bernard Shaw in the estate agent's office. But what is more apposite is that the advent of prosperity to both these great writers did not in any way reduce their activity or their quality;

it merely gave them the time to write. It did, it is true, awaken in the mind of Shaw fanciful apprehensions that he would be ruined by taxation, but these are fears shared by others who do not have the justification of genius for occasional eccentricities.

The conclusion of all this is that the author today is no better off than he ever was, is not working under the improved conditions that civilization should have bought, and – if he wants it – should be able to receive sensible support to enable him to write books of quality. I say, 'if he wants it'; I do not believe in forcible feeding. Many authors resent the very suggestion of patronage, and this attitude should be respected. But where public patronage is concerned they can reflect that a willingness to take support from the state and society is not ignominious or humiliating – if the conditions are right. I have noticed with irony that many of the strongest opponents of subsidy for the arts come from worlds where large profits are accepted from government contracts. Nobody regards this as demeaning. Nor is it demeaning that a man should be entitled to render a service to his fellow men with their support.

The question of private patronage is a difficult one. There is current a strong belief that more of this is obtainable and should be obtained. As Chairman of the Arts Council I welcome financial support from all quarters. If the Arts Council subsidy were extracted in the torture chambers of the Tower of London, I should deplore the methods but reluctantly accept the proceeds. And an increase in private subsidy is a very healthy thing. The state should not have a monopoly of patronage. However carefully organized any organization devoted to support the arts, it is a good thing that the practitioners should be provided with alternative sources of help. We do not want a theatre totally dominated by subsidy; nor do we want to restrict the exhibition of painting to public galleries. In the world of literature the private sector does infinitely more than the public sector – reversing the balance existing in the other arts.

So far as the customer is concerned, there is very little call for subsidy. Publishers can be pretty well relied upon to publish any worthwhile book that is sent to them, and certainly, once its merits are recognized, no subsidy is needed to encourage the publication. Very occasionally a book of special quality presents commercial problems. It may be exceptionally expensive to produce, or may expose the publisher to a special commercial risk because of its limited appeal, and yet it ought to be published as a contribution to learning or letters. In such cases the practice now adopted by the Arts Council for making grants to publishers – and there are very few of them each year – is, I think, undoubtedly right, and even more so is the practice of encouraging translation.

One of the shortcomings, perhaps unavoidable in English commercial publishing, is the English version of important foreign books. A subsidy to help the unpromising commercial situation is appropriate and important.

The question of subsidizing an author is, of course, much more difficult. The hideous question of value judgments, of the right choice, arises. The Arts Council's experience in the six years since it established a Literature Panel has not been wholly fortunate. We have received vigorous criticism for our awards and our failure to make awards. The TLS has played a leading part in the periodic onslaughts. This is right and good. Nothing is more damaging than complacency on the part of a grant-making body. There have, of course, been authors we should have subsidized, and there has been ground for legitimate misgivings about some of the subsidies that we have given. Our Literature Panel has, I think, been as representative as we could make it. Often when criticism is directed to the constitution of a panel, and the absence of particular dignitaries is noted, it is without knowledge of their refusal to participate. Many writers are too busy, and properly take the view that their function is writing and not serving on committees. I hope that those who have taken this view will, nevertheless, reflect again if invitations are extended to them, and will join their many distinguished colleagues who have enlisted without demur. There is an important public function concerned and, while no one can reproach them if they do not join, we can applaud their devotion to the cause if they do.

Arts Council proceedings, I may say, are not tedious. They are infinitely varied and splendidly controversial. But we have certainly learnt something from the experience of the years. For instance, we became increasingly dubious about the literary prize. My own feeling (remembering the brutal treatment of poor Proust when awarded the Goncourt) had always been that while it was a good thing for some public body not concerned in the business of making grants to provide an occasional handsome prize – which after all adds to the general revenue of authors – it was far better for a grant-making body to avoid classifying authors by the award of prizes, and to organize their subsidy by way of grants and bursaries to writers who needed the money for particular projects. In short, it is not necessary or desirable for the Arts Council to say that X is better than Y. It is, I think, highly desirable for the Arts Council to say that Y – an author of established merit or obvious promise – should have a grant of realistic size to enable him to write a book or to try to write his book.

And what of the other conditions that must prevail for respectable subsidy? I have pronounced them so often that they have become tedious in the repetition. First and foremost, that no condition should attach which affects the nature or quality of the writing. Subsidy must not be a fetter on freedom of thought or expression. The writer – and the artist in any other field – must write and paint and compose as he wishes – and as if the subsidy had not existed. This is the paramount consideration. It does not need to be argued. In its absence subsidy is disreputable, and we would be better without it.

I noticed with distress a correspondence recently when an author was boiling with indignation because he thought – as it happened mistakenly – that the Arts Council required him to publish in his book an acknowledgement of his grant or bursary as a condition of the award. It was explained we had no such rule – and I hope we never have such a rule. Our naïve belief was that it might be helpful to the author to indicate that his merit had been recognized by a subsidy. Also – and with equal naïvety – we believe that the public might like to identify the works which we supported; but certainly no author should be required to carry the brand of an Arts Council or any other subsidy if he did not wish to.

The Arts Council Reports show the range and extents of our grants. I do not believe that we are yet of real importance to literature in this country, but our value will grow with the availability of more money. We have supported a number of deserving writers, and over the years, I think, it will emerge that the money has been well spent. Some will be ungrateful and inconsiderate – and will fail to become geniuses. This is a possibility that we should view with composure. No effective subsidizing organization can avoid waste. The importance of sensible subsidy is that, by spreading its benefit as widely as is reasonably possible, we seek to avoid the neglect of an important and needy writer. If, in so doing, we bestow subsidy on some writers less important but equally needy, this must be an acceptable risk.

I recommend to those with built-in prejudice against state subsidy a careful examination of all the Arts Council's Annual Reports for the past few years before they utter condemnation. The Arts Council does not replace the traditional private patron. It cannot be a substitute for the nobleman who in the eighteenth century would be attracted to the brilliant son of an indigent clergyman and provide him with his education and the opportunity to exploit his talent. This is personal patronage which hardly survives in the present day. It has been replaced by the state scholarship and the county grant, and a great number of other impersonal sources of support which, since they involve a lesser element of caprice are, in my view, better, juster, and more suitable for a modern world.

I hope that the subsidy of literature through the Arts Council or other public means will continue and will expand. To the many authors who are dissatisfied because they have failed to procure grants, and who naturally feel that their cases have not received full and proper consideration, I would offer the small comfort that many of us are conscious that no machine is perfect, and that its operators should be constantly on the alert for its improvement, notwithstanding the strenuous efforts we already exert.

(*The Times Literary Supplement*, October 9, 1970)

7. A Fair Deal for Authors

Authors in Britain are living under a library system which works injustice to them. It seems to me as plain as the nose on my face that it is a social wrong to allow a book still in copyright to be borrowed from a public library (either free or on payment) without payment of any kind to the living author. A great deal of sophistry has been wasted in obscuring this simple situation.

It is difficult to diagnose the reason for the hostility to the schemes for a Public Lending Right. It is not that people hate authors or wish them to be treated harshly. Nor is it a failure to recognize that the rewards of authorship are pitifully inadequate, and that the advent of a just library system would do something – although not all that much – to redress the balance.

There is, I think, a complex of reasons. First and foremost the whole conception of copyright – which is a sophisticated legal conception – is instinctively understood by very few people. Their notion of legal property in relation to a book is that it is a chattel owned by the purchaser. The idea that a subsidiary legal right reposes in some remote person in relation to an article in one's own household – or on a library shelf – is alien.

It must be remembered that the theory of copyright is, by the timetable of legal conceptions, a modern one. It was not until 1774, in the famous case of Donaldson *v.* Beckett, that the nature and extent of copyright was determined in this country. Advanced legal systems such as the Roman and the Roman-Dutch systems knew nothing of copyright. The great classical authors would have been agreeably astonished to receive a payment for any multiplication of their works. But the idea of copyright made sense only after the introduction of printing. And even today the idea that an incorporeal right of this character should be as inviolate as any other right of property is not easily received in untutored minds.

It is only in a very modern society, where the artist – however unpalatable the notion – discovers he can protect himself only by membership of an organization in a solidly united front, that due respect is paid to artistic rights when they can be enforced by the pressures of association. But authors are ill-suited for trade unionism. The creative writer is essentially an individualist. Distraction from his gift for the purposes of professional organization is distasteful and bothersome. Hence, the unions of authorship have never had the strength or efficacy of the Musicians' Union or Equity.

This is not the fault of the untiring officers of the organizations involved. It is due to a belief, based to some extent on the quality of pessimism found in all artists, that nothing can be permanently effective against the rigours of a harsh world. And their defeatist attitude is, of course, constantly finding support and confirmation from the world's behaviour.

It is not the purpose of this campaign to drive a wedge between authors and their public. Its purpose is to seek to convince people that the Public Lending Right should be bestowed on authors not as an act of kindliness or generosity, but as, in the words of Mr Angus Wilson, 'a matter of justice.'

Of course, there are other contentions to be dealt with. There is a superstitious fear that the free lending library will be interfered with, and that someone may have to pay a penny, twopence or threepence to borrow a book. In our present society most people would view this possibility with sensible composure. On the other hand, deep concern that the 'free library' should be maintained is a viewpoint worthy of respect – demonstrating the right set of values. But if the cost of the libraries requires a fee it will not be because of the Public Lending Right, which is merely a proper expense to be met out of the libraries' budgets in exactly the same way as the cost of cleaning or repairs. It would be interesting to observe the reactions of a cleaner or a workman repairing the roof who was asked to provide services free of charge in order to preserve free lending.

Another familiar argument is that no scheme can be introduced which is just – that rich authors will get much richer and poor authors will remain almost as poor. Strangely enough, this is an argument introduced by people who are not by nature revolutionaries. They do not wish to despoil the rich. They would regard as madness any egalitarian schemes for ensuring that the more prosperous stockbrokers should be penalized by a differential commission in favour of their poorer brethren. It is equally demented to prevent authors receiving their legal due in a noncommunist society, because that due may provide additional benefits to the successful. The redistribution of wealth will not be achieved by depriving authors of their Public Lending Right, and the majority of people in this country recently demonstrated that they are quite happy if it should not be achieved at all.

It is wrong to minimize the difficulties, or to pretend that the scheme will not involve administrative effort and some unavoidable anomalies. I am amply satisfied, from a careful study of this matter over the years, that a scheme can be devised which will involve no unfair burden on libraries and will restore justice to writers. It will have its problems. It certainly will not operate in terms of pure justice – it will not bestow particular benefits on good authors as opposed to bad authors. It will bestow benefits according to popularity – a criterion we now accept in every field. This criterion is acceptable to authors, although they are happy also to accept a regulator to ensure that proportionately a royalty is paid at a decreasing rate according to popularity.

The maintenance of good authors who do not enjoy public demand is not the primary purpose of Public Lending Right. A civilized society must find – and increasingly is finding – ways of dealing with this question. But this is quite a different issue from that of restoring to authors a legal right of which they have been robbed for generations.

(Preface to *The Public Lending Right: A Matter of Justice*, an anthology edited by Richard Findlater, André Deutsch, January 1971)

8. *The Arts Council and the New Activists*

The Arts Council's activities are not widely publicized, although everything we do is exposed to the cleansing light of day. The public on the whole is not passionately interested in the Council as such, although very interested and each day becoming more so in the actual activities which we promote or generate. But a startling exception has been the New Activities Committee of the Arts Council, which has prompted more newspaper and public comment than all the rest of our exertions put together.

It is my purpose to offer some explanations to the public which, I hope, will redeem the Arts Council of suspicions and accusations that it has taken leave of its corporate senses, and is engaged in a process of nihilistic destructivism, astonishing for individuals hitherto of such impeccable antecedents.

First, may I reassure the many correspondents both to me and to newspapers that there is not the remotest prospect that the Arts Council will pay the fine of any individual – young or old, male or female – who has committed offences in the vicinity of the American Embassy or elsewhere. The Arts Council's funds are to promote art, not crime! The public who have burst blood vessels over this matter must not regard the Arts Council as wholly responsible for their neuroses.

First, our public record entitles us to the benefit of the doubt – a very large doubt, I venture to think – that we should entertain any such proposal. Secondly, a simple inquiry from the Council would have explained how the whole matter arose. Like so much in life, it arose from our incorrigible determination to do something where inaction and apathy would leave us safe and secure and free from abuse.

Some eighteen months ago the Arts Council received, and went on to be bombarded with, applications for grant-aid from what to them were unfamiliar activities: arts laboratories, theatre groups, loosely knit bodies of young people operating in halls and basements were asking for financial aid to support and maintain their various activities.

Many of these came under no clearly identifiable Arts Council heading. They were not precisely drama or music or literature or belonging to the visual arts, but it was clear that there were surface stirrings all over the country. And it was clear that their practitioners took them seriously.

The Arts Council dealt with a number of them through the medium of its existing panels for the four particular arts I have mentioned, but a large accumulation remained inappropriate for such treatment. The matter was discussed by the Council, and we decided that they reflected sufficient interesting activity to justify a detailed inquiry.

We as a Council did not know quite what these young people were doing, what their intentions and aspirations were, and whether there was anything in their work that should be encouraged and even preserved. Clearly there was something approaching a new move. We decided, therefore, to set up a Committee which we called the New Activities Committee. Its membership was, in my view, both appropriate and impressive.

Among its original members were Michael Astor (formerly a Conservative MP) who has acted as Chairman throughout and who has discharged what, in the event, has been a task of considerable difficulty, with great sympathy, understanding and integrity. Others included the Earl of Harewood, Sir Edward Boyle MP, and Sir Joseph Lockwood, the Chairman of EMI.

The Committee – as happens with long-standing committees – changed its personnel as members became unavailable and new members were required. From the Council were added Peter Hall, the distinguished theatrical director; Jack Lambert, the literary editor of the *Sunday Times*, and – at the instigation of the Committee itself – a number of the new activists.

Difficulties inevitably arose: the new activists did not think as did their older colleagues; the problems of communication and interpretership were considerable. Much time was occupied, for instance, in discussing whether the proceedings of the Committee should be tape-recorded in view of the new members' obvious mistrust of any record or minutes produced by a human being and not a machine.

In fact, the new activists movement is characterized as perhaps one would expect in this age, by its superior confidence in machinery over people. Moreover, many of the young people clearly did not like the Arts Council and did their business with it only because of the allure of its money and its premises. Of this, with great candour, they made no secret. They produced magazines containing caricatures of the Arts Council's hapless chairman, depicting him as an octopus, of which his only comment was that the tentacles were too few and too short.

But Mr Astor and his Committee soldiered on. Indifferent to insult, innuendo, and intrigue, they are proceeding to do what they were instructed to do. The Committee was set up solely to investigate and produce a report. And this we earnestly hope they will achieve within the next few weeks. The Council will receive from the Committee a report and recommendations about all these matters.

The activities of the new Committee to date have been laboratory activities. They will tell us, we earnestly hope, whether their research has been worthwhile and what emerges from it. These activities by themselves constitute neither an endorsement nor a criticism of the matters they have been inspecting. Nor in the end will the Council's recommendations necessarily amount to either of such judgments. What we will decide is whether in all this fret and ferment there is something worthy of public support from public funds. If so, how much of it so qualifies and in what fashion (if any) it should receive further support.

Some of it may turn out to have been exhibitionist nonsense; some of it to relate to coteries so small as to have no public claim; some of it may – for all we know – be new and fresh and vital. This we hope our committee will tell us. If it emerges that there are things worth supporting after they have gone through the sieve of the committee's deliberations, the money we have spent on this report (£15,000) will, in my view, have been well spent.

If the conclusion is that there is nothing worth supporting – although there may still be much of merit in the activities – the money will, in my view, have been well wasted. It would have been very wrong for a council whose function is to maintain the arts of all generations to have turned their back on manifestations as serious and widespread as these new activities.

Nothing that is totally sincere can be totally ridiculous, and the fact that their votaries may have hair of Elizabethan length or skirts too short to be noticeable is not a matter which affects the Arts Council in its judgments. The stances over the generations have affronted many worthy but lesser people. Our job, so far as it can be humanly discharged – and this is a serious limitation – is to identify and sustain the artist.

And on the question of the fine and other recommendations about which I had almost forgotten to furnish an explanation, these were made neither by the New Activities Committee nor by the Council. They were the recommendations of a group of young activists presided over by a regional organizer, and obviously made – so far as the fine was concerned – as much to twist the tail of the Arts Council as the general public. They must be congratulated on a substantial measure of success in this objective, although they must now endure the disappointment that a crude political manœuvre – their recommendation in relation to the fine – needs to receive the endorsement of a body whose principal quality is that it is free from political influence both inside and out.

(*Evening Standard*, April 2, 1970)

9. *Obscenity and the Arts*

I think it right to see the area in which we are involved because I believe that one may exaggerate the extent of this problem. At the Arts Council I receive, I should think, not more than six letters a year from people complaining that one or other of our activities is, in their view, obscene, or indecent, or pornographic. It is very rarely, I may say, that there is not some basis for what is written in the letter. Nearly always, when I receive a letter, my intention is to write a fighting reply. When I send for the file on the matter almost invariably it becomes extremely difficult to provide a fighting reply. I should like to give one instance which I was proposing to submit to some magazine that has literary compositions inviting the readers to suggest the sort of reply which might be furnished in the circumstances, because I could not think of one.

This was the case of an extremely progressive and most valuable theatre which had decided to put on, for the attendance of children, a play which hitherto had been presented for adults – a perfectly proper and highly appropriate activity. But for the purpose of the children's production they had decided to salt the play with a number of obscenities that did not appear in the adult version. I should like to invite the readers of the *New Statesman*, or some other literary magazine, to supply the Chairman of the Arts Council with a defensive reply that he could send in respect of that particular operation.

The other side of that coin is that when I dipped my pen in vitriol in order to write a letter to the organization concerned – indeed we wrote a very forthright and fighting letter – the reply came that there had been no complaint from any parent of any child who attended. This I think is a highly relevant consideration. We have to remember the audiences with which we are dealing and the circumstances in which these productions are presented. We have to remember that, whatever our views may be on this matter (my views are very simple: my favourite author is Jane Austen, and undoubtedly my favourite dramatist is the late William Shakespeare), the fact that we may have rather simple tastes does not mean that they are universally shared.

Invariably, my Lords, when I go to the theatre today to what may be called an *avant garde* play, I observe a very startling phenomenon. I am invariably shocked – my hair stands on end more than it normally does – but I observe that while what is being said is, to me, highly shocking, no such reaction is produced on any other member of the audience. I look to the left and to the right, and I see that they accept with absolute composure what are, to me, highly disagreeable utterances. I was brought up in a household where it was absolutely wrong to use even such a mild word as 'bloody'. I never heard that word used within the confines of my home. Yet I find myself sitting through plays in which the most vigorous physiological obscenities are uttered, minute by minute, by every character, and I find that I am completely attuned to them. They no longer strike me as being in any way startling or unusual, or as having some special feature.

It is clear that, with habit, practices can change. But is it necessarily the case that in more repressive societies one necessarily has the better morality? I have a recollection that in the home town of the Mahdi, the gentleman who got involved with General Gordon, there was the agreeable position that any kind of marital infidelity was punished by death. Yet I do not think that people searching for the most moral community in the world would have chosen that particular one. It has always been presented to the world as an instance of hideous immorality. So it is necessary for us to reflect very carefully before we embark on changes in areas which are extraordinarily delicate and difficult. It would be absolutely wrong, as the Paymaster General said, to use public money for public corruption. As a simple axiom, this cannot be the subject of dispute. But how can one operate this? The circumstances in which one decides that activities are corrupt present problems of great difficulty.

In the Arts Council we set up a working party to investigate the obscenity laws, and I may say that it was a salutary experience to see how it developed. We called together a conference of many people concerned with writing, publishing and literary matters, and I presided. I recommended strongly that the one thing the working party should not do was to recommend the total abolition of the obscenity laws, on the practical ground that nobody was going to abolish them. Nothing could have acted as a greater encouragement to the working party than that admonition, for their report emerged as a forthright recommendation that all the obscenity laws should be abolished. We received a very cogent and splendidly written report, demonstrating that, in the view of the working party which prepared it, the obscenity laws were inappropriate, served no useful purpose and in fact were positively vicious. We read the Report and it is fair to say that we did not go all the way with it. Obviously it made a prima facie case, but we felt that this was a matter which needed a good deal more evidence to be adduced.

Much importance was attached to the fact that in Denmark the abolition of the obscenity laws was alleged to coincide with a material decline in convictions for sexual offences. I must confess that I found this a little difficult to credit. It may be the case in Denmark, but I find it difficult to square this with the fact that in many grave cases of sexual offences in this country part of the evidence adduced is that the man convicted was in possession of a considerable quantity of obscene literature. It is difficult to square that fact with the belief that the abolition of the obscenity laws and more easy provision of obscene literature would produce fewer sexual offences. In any event, my Lords, the report was a serious and mature contribution to the discussion. The Council decided that we would not adopt the Report but would send it to the Home Secretary and ask him to have a look at it, to see whether it was appropriate to set up a fuller investigation to take wider evidence on a wider front. Nothing has happened in the matter.

It is my view that the premature abolition of the obscenity laws would cause difficulties not envisaged by the working party. Their thoughts naturally turned to what one might call serious literature. I do not believe that if the obscenity laws were abolished in respect of the publications of serious and responsible publishers, anyone would come to any harm. But what they had forgotten was that there are large areas of potential danger elsewhere – even, for instance, in the newspapers, of which I can speak with a little authority.

My Lords, I do not think that anyone seeing the newspapers of today would say that it was wise to abolish the obscenity laws and leave everyone the right to publish what he liked in newspapers which appear on everyone's table without any thought of control or any sort of regulation. Certainly it could not be wise to do it without grave and mature thought, and with rather more deliberate calculation than our Committee had been able to give. I mention this as the sort of difficulty to which this problem gives rise, and I again emphasize the desirability of making sure that the problem is not accentuated by premature action. It is a small problem. The Arts Council subsidizes some seventy repertory theatres. The complaints received amount to about six letters a year, and no more. It is evident that the problem is not merely trifling but almost insignificant as a serious aspect of the work we have to do. That is not to say that it ought to be ignored, but it certainly should not be exaggerated.

I should like to say a word on one other topic with which we are enormously concerned in connection with broadcasting in general. There is, I think, a much more important matter to be considered than the question of pornography and obscenity. There is, I believe, a view spreading that programmes should be presented according to the whim and desire of the producer, without any serious or special regard to the truth of the matters that are being presented. These are not being presented to the public as something which is casual or haphazard or accidental. It is a deliberate trend of opinion today, quite deliberate and honourable, which says that the presentation of a matter according to the viewpoint of a particular individual is defensible and should be permitted, provided that an opportunity is given for an alternative point of view to be presented at some other time. I regard this as both nonsensical and dangerous. I do not think that we can abrogate truth because later someone may be given an opportunity to nail the lie. As I say, I regard this doctrine as both nonsensical and dangerous; I think it is a preposterous doctrine to enunciate. I have had an opportunity of expressing my views in correspondence on the subject. But it is a fact that this view is widely spread, and it is a growing point of view.

This same view is associated with another point which is equally dangerous, and that is a spurious claim for liberty. There is of course a claim for liberty to express a man's view on a particular subject, but that claim becomes something else if it becomes a claim for the liberty to express views presented in whatever form he chooses to present it, so that, however vulgar, however cheap, however gross or however stupid the presentation may be, the author of this presentation argues that it should not be stopped and he should not be controlled because that would be an interference with his personal liberty. My Lords, there is no liberty of any kind to violate the public screen with presentations of a vulgar, gross, coarse, and repulsive character. This is an unknown liberty, and the claim that is now being made for it is an unknown claim that should not be encouraged.

(Speech in the House of Lords, February 3, 1971)

10. Pornography in Britain

My Lords, this is an interesting point at which to intervene in the debate. I apologize to the noble Earl, Lord Longford, for the fact that, as I had a commitment with a Parliamentary Committee, I heard only a portion of his opening address. But I should like to say this. I yield to no one in my admiration for the noble Earl. In making that remark, may I say that it is not designed to embarrass him, but because it has some relevance to what I am going to say. The noble Earl is a very unusual person; he is a good man, set on making a good and a better world. This, if I may say so, is not so common that we may ignore the phenomenon or fail to admire and respect it. But it may be that someone with, perhaps, rather fewer of the admirable qualities than he possesses could make a better assessment of the murky scene that the noble Earl surveyed.

My Lords, the noble Earl opened his remarks with the assertion – derived from the old debating society which we all used to attend – that pornography has increased, is increasing and ought to be diminished. With the final tag of that admonition no one would disagree. Obviously, pornography ought to be diminished, if we can find means of diminishing it. That, by definition, cannot be anything but a good thing. But I venture to doubt whether pornography has increased to that extent, or whether it is increasing to the extent that the noble Earl envisages. I wonder whether his researches have not been altogether too specialized and rarefied to arrive at a really true appraisal of the situation.

Of course, there are the strip tease clubs. In the immense preoccupations of my own life I have never had the fortunate opportunity of attending them. Perhaps, when I am relieved of certain public obligations, I can indulge my private pleasures more copiously. But strip tease clubs do exist; that is quite plain if you go to Soho to visit restaurants, as I do. But they do not seem to me to have proliferated. In fact, I am happy to say the restaurants have encroached on their territory in several areas, and a number of clubs have closed down. If you go to Soho to visit a particular restaurant you will now, my Lords, be privileged to observe that in places where there were erstwhile strip tease clubs there are respectable Italian or French restaurants. I venture to doubt whether there has been any great increase in strip tease clubs in that area, but I have not carried out a Gallup poll.

In relation to the London theatre, some three years ago or a little longer, we engaged ourselves in what I thought was a rather splendid emancipation of the theatre from the thraldom of a censorship, which was not an onerous, or a cruel, or an unintelligent censorship, but one which was bitterly resented by the dramatists. We took a step forward in favour of liberty and tolerance. It was greatly appreciated, and I think it has been rewarded. I venture to think that I attend the London theatre as often as any Member of your Lordships' House. If I may say so, it is very rarely indeed that I encounter any Member of your Lordships' House there. I make this point, not to draw attention to my own virtue, but because of its relevance in relation to assessing the situation. I do not think the London theatre today is more obscene than it was. I do not think it is obscene. If an American visitor arrived in London today, and made a representative tour of the London theatres, I do not think that the quality that would particularly commend itself to him would be the obscenity of the theatre. I think it would be the splendour of some of the productions and the great quality of some of the acting. The fact that we have contrived to achieve one of the great theatres in the world, which is lauded loudly on all sides, is in part the product of the new atmosphere of tolerance and liberty. We must be very slow indeed before we take steps that may endanger those splendid qualities.

Where else is this proliferation of pornography to be found? We are told about films. I see one Member of your Lordships' House who knows more about the cinema than anyone else – the noble Lord, Lord Harlech, who is Chairman of the Board of British Film Censors. I venture to say – and I invite contradiction from him – that in relation to the ordinary respectable cinema, the cinema to which people go and purchase their tickets at the box office without suffering possible embarrassment from being detected by their neighbours on entering, far from there being a deterioration in moral quality, the moral quality is in fact improving considerably. The films which are today attracting the public and creating large box office returns and substantial profits are films of simple morality – sometimes to a point which to some viewers is approaching the positively nauseating. The fact remains that these are moral films: films like *Ryan's Daughter*, *The Railway Children*, *Melody* and *Love Story*. I could retail them by the dozen, because I have some professional preoccupation with these matters. These are not obscene films. There is not an increase in obscenity.

Of course people are sneaking through the Customs blue films made by poor deprived creatures for other deprived creatures because their instability and insecurity needs some assistance of this kind, and showing them in cellars in Soho. But can one say that this is a sufficiently important social phenomenon to exercise the attention of your Lordships for more than a second? The police and the Customs have ample powers to deal with this matter, if they are minded to do so. If they do not take steps to launch prosecutions, that is up to them. One of the difficulties they have to encounter is that prosecution in relation to these matters is one of appalling difficulty. It is not so much a matter of definition. Of course no human being – and certainly not twelve human beings, which makes them twelve times less effective than one – can possible determine whether a particular piece of writing or literature is calculated to corrupt another human being. As a legal and social problem, this is insoluble. But this need not worry anyone acquainted with prosecutions in this area. Because what a jury does is not to sit down and discuss the fine points of the judge's direction to them. They say to themselves, 'Is this a filthy piece of work?' And on the whole, having heard the admonitions addressed to them, they decide one way or the other. If the noble and learned Lord, the former Lord Chancellor, Lord Gardiner, was one of the distinguished defenders of a work, the work concerned would be almost certain of acquittal, because the jury would appreciate through seeing him that that very fact exonerated the work from any possibility of being tainted in any way. I urge upon the noble Earl to consider whether all this fuss is really worth while.

I think that there is an importation into this country of a considerable quantity of what might be called filth. This I do not regard as important. I think it is restricted to a few specialist clubs and cinemas and to my mind it does not have an effect upon our society worthy of this elaborate discussion.

May I say this to the noble Earl in all conviction? I do not believe that the young people of this country are any worse today than were the young people twenty or thirty years ago. I do not think that the cream of our youth are being tainted by pornography. I do not think that the flower of England are being tainted by pornography. I know that the young people who come into my own office as articled clerks are better than at any other time in my experience. The young people reading at the universities and going to the Bar have a shrewder assessment of the moral problem than I have ever encountered in my life. I believe that it would be profoundly discouraging to them if a message goes out from this House telling them that they are saturated in pornography; that their standards are bad and evil, and that they need to have special regard to the dangers confronting them. This, in my view, would be a very real danger.

I agree entirely with what the noble Viscount, Lord Eccles, said. This is a matter where we are living in a world of imperfect standards. I believe that there are more dangerous things than pornography. Greed, cruelty, avarice and many other things are greater dangers to our society than pornography. I am not sure that the best advice we give to our people is that everyone should stand on his own feet. I am not sure that any of these qualities are things that make for a better world; but I am sure that the moral danger confronting us at this second is not the danger of pornography.

I would particularly urge on the noble Earl one consideration. I hope that he will not set up a private investigatory committee. This would be a most unfortunate conception. To suggest in such a delicate area as this that one set of human beings should arrogate to themselves, without Governmental authority, the task of investigating another set of human beings, seems to me most unfortunate.

I am a libertarian. I am totally in favour of tolerance. If the noble Earl sets up his committee, I shall take no steps at all to interfere with its work – I give him that assurance. But I think it would be extremely ill-advised for him to consider doing such a thing. These are, in my view, areas where the minimum of Government interference is desirable, and a total absence of private interference. I do not think that people should investigate what their neighbours are doing. I do not think that people should investigate what some unfortunate wretch is compelled to read because of some compulsion beyond his own understanding. I am absolutely convinced that things are not so bad as they are made out. I am absolutely convinced that unless we are very careful, if we allow this tide of feeling to sweep us forward in an atmosphere of relative unreason, things will be a good deal worse.

(Speech in the House of Lords, April 21, 1971)

Postscript

That, for good or ill, this book has seen the light of day is attributable to the determination of its publisher, my friend André Deutsch. But, although I was unconvinced about the publication, I am not sorry that the book has been published. It does place within a single compass my views on a number of subjects, which represent a reasonable cross-section of my views on most subjects. If one has attained a certain degree of public notoriety, it is desirable to make one's position known. I have not suffered any special misrepresentation; on the whole, I have been fortunate in the public comment about my modest exertions. But, these papers state authentically in my own words the things I very genuinely and often very fervently believed and, with a few rare instances, continue to believe. Reading them again, I am surprised how little my opinions have changed since I wrote or spoke any particular sentiment or opinion.

In isolated instances I would revise my views. A closer view of the working of the newspaper industry causes me to doubt whether direct subsidy is a possible solution, although I would still prefer it to the disappearance of an important part of the Press. But, a few such areas apart, there is no opinion that I particularly wish to change – although I would have welcomed an opportunity, denied to me by pressures of time, to clothe my thoughts in more finished language.

These papers touch on many aspects of a busy life over the last few years, when it assumed some public role. Principally, my public life has been concerned with and concentrated on the Arts Council, and a good deal of what you have just read relates to the Council and to the arts in general. But, I do and have done other things, and the book provides some comment on these also. It only remains for me to thank my friend Noel Annan for his kind and far too generous preface, and to hope that my readers will have found something of interest in the preceding pages.

January 3, 1972